Inscribed for James Wallace
with the authors best
wishes

DEC' 02

POLICING THE PENINSULA
(1850 - 2000)

(A Photographic Celebration of
Westcountry Policing over the last 150 years)

POLICING THE PENINSULA
(1850 - 2000)

(A Photographic Celebration of
Westcountry Policing over the last 150 years)

By SIMON DELL, MBE

FOREST PUBLISHING
(In association with the Devon & Cornwall Constabulary)

First published in 2000 by FOREST PUBLISHING
(in association with the Devon & Cornwall Constabulary),
Woodstock, Liverton, Newton Abbot, Devon TQ12 6JJ

British Library Cataloguing in Publication Data.

A catalogue record for this book is available from the British Library.

ISBN   0 9527297 9 2

Forest Publishing

Design, layout and typeset by:
Simon Dell, MBE

Editorial by:
Mike Lang and Wendy Roderick Hake

Printed and bound in Great Britain by:
The Latimer Trend Group, Plymouth, Devon PL6 7PL

Cover illustration:
A map of the outline of the area policed by the Devon & Cornwall Constabulary, with officers of the Torquay division circa 1899 (see page 97) in the area of Devon, and officers at Camborne circa 1925 in the area of Cornwall.

Dedication

This book is dedicated to
those who never joined the police service,
but became just as much a part of it ...

Policemen's wives everywhere.

Constable Frank Burrow's marriage to Miss Milly Blee in 1932,
at Paignton.

(Mrs Gillian Lugg)

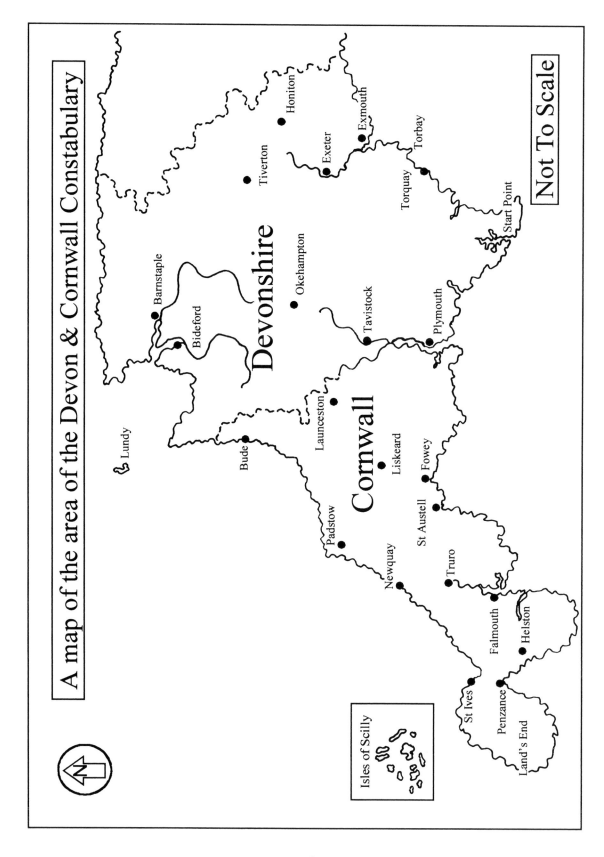

A map of the area of the Devon & Cornwall Constabulary

Not To Scale

Devonshire

Cornwall

Lundy

Barnstaple

Bideford

Tiverton

Honiton

Exeter

Exmouth

Torbay

Torquay

Start Point

Okehampton

Tavistock

Plymouth

Launceston

Bude

Liskeard

Fowey

Padstow

St Austell

Newquay

Truro

Falmouth

Helston

St Ives

Penzance

Land's End

Isles of Scilly

N

Contents

Acknowledgements

As with my previous book, *The Beat on Western Dartmoor*, the support of the Chief Constable has been essential in being able to produce such a photographic history of the force; I trust that it does not disappoint him.

Part of the task of preparing this book involved the services of the Force Photographic Unit situated at Headquarters. In fact, the enormous amount of help which I received from members of that department was overwhelming: whether it was through copying borrowed pictures or being allowed to ransack their archives, that support proved to be an essential part of this book's existence. In particular, special thanks go to Sally Robinson for spending so much of her free time in the evenings on producing the layout and design for the front cover.

Three years of collecting photographs from pensioners and serving officers alike has shown beyond doubt that pride and commitment to the service is as strong as ever. Most of the photographs in the book have come from pensioners and private collections, and I am grateful indeed for the loan of precious mementoes of previous generations - too many contributors to mention each by name, but all have been so supportive and interested in playing some part in this story of policing.

The majority of the helmet plate badges have been taken from the vast collections of Jeff Cowdell, Dave Wilkinson and Vic Denyer of the Police Insignia Collectors Association, and my thanks go to them for their help in providing photographs and research material for me to use. Also to my brother, Constable Christopher Dell, of the Metropolitan Police for his visits to their Police Museum and National Archives of Badges on my behalf.

Finally, I should like to say "Thankyou" to all of those people who have helped me in so many ways, for without their support these photographs would have remained unseen and the efforts of those portrayed in them might have gone unrecorded.

Author's Note

Whilst every care has been taken in preparing and researching this book, it is only reasonable that the effect of time and human frailty should be taken into account. If a name is spelt or recalled incorrectly then an apology is offered in advance. Where an opinion is expressed, it is that of the author and not of the Devon & Cornwall Constabulary.

Whilst the Devon & Cornwall Constabulary share the copyright to this publication, Constable Simon Dell, MBE exercises his right to be known as 'The Author'. All profits from the sale of this book, incidentally, are to be donated to the Devon & Cornwall Constabulary Widows and Orphans Compassionate Fund charity.

Photographs where sources are not acknowledged are from either the author's collection or the archives of the Devon & Cornwall Constabulary museum.

Foreword

The Chief Constable

Entering a new millennium provides a useful opportunity to review the past, for it is only by reflecting upon what has been achieved previously that we can strive to improve our service to the public in the future. Throughout the last two centuries the police service has had to alter and adapt to meet enormous changes in society and the demands which it makes of us. This book catalogues in photographs much of that change throughout the Westcountry, at a time when we, in the Devon & Cornwall Constabulary, look ahead and focus our attention on how best to meet the demands of the future.

As Chief Constable I am proud to have steered the force through some of the more recent aspects of that progress and development during the past two decades, as we changed how we did things in order to improve our quality of service to the public of our counties, cities and islands. As the police service is developed and taken forward into the new century, it is through the pages of this book that we can look back, perhaps with a little unashamed sentimentality, at our policing forebears and be assured that change has always been inevitable - but never at the pace we experience currently as we make the most of new science and technology. So long as we use current developments wisely then we, in the police service, can be assured that, by working together, hand-in-hand, with the communities we serve, the future is promising indeed. My congratulations are due to Constable Simon Dell,MBE (and those who have assisted him) for this splendid photographic history of the development of *Policing the Peninsula*.

Sir John S. Evans Q.P.M LL.B
Chief Constable
President of the Association of Chief Police Officers
Police Headquarters
Exeter
1st January 2000

THE DEVON & CORNWALL CONSTABULARY
'FAMILY TREE'

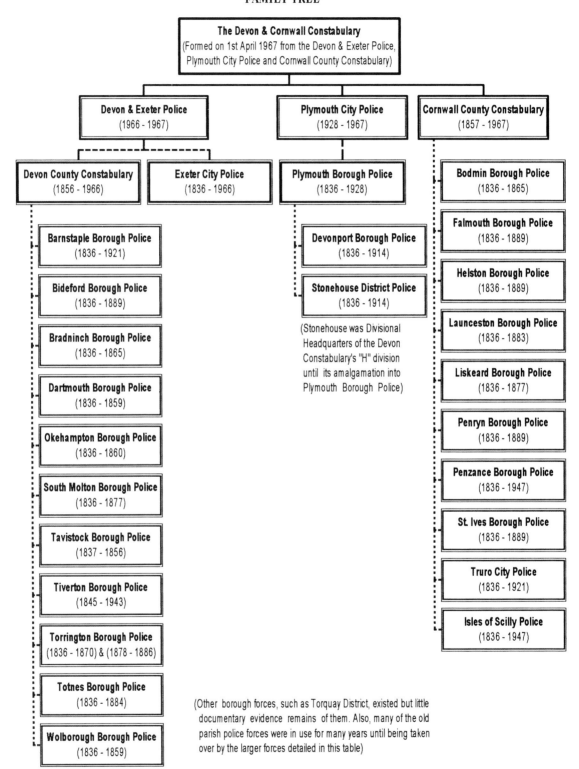

The Devon & Cornwall Constabulary
(Formed on 1st April 1967 from the Devon & Exeter Police,
Plymouth City Police and Cornwall County Constabulary)

Devon & Exeter Police
(1966 - 1967)

Plymouth City Police
(1928 - 1967)

Cornwall County Constabulary
(1857 - 1967)

Devon County Constabulary
(1856 - 1966)

Exeter City Police
(1836 - 1966)

Plymouth Borough Police
(1836 - 1928)

Bodmin Borough Police
(1836 - 1865)

Barnstaple Borough Police
(1836 - 1921)

Devonport Borough Police
(1836 - 1914)

Falmouth Borough Police
(1836 - 1889)

Bideford Borough Police
(1836 - 1889)

Stonehouse District Police
(1836 - 1914)

Helston Borough Police
(1836 - 1889)

Bradninch Borough Police
(1836 - 1865)

(Stonehouse was Divisional
Headquarters of the Devon
Constabulary's "H" division
until its amalgamation into
Plymouth Borough Police)

Launceston Borough Police
(1836 - 1883)

Dartmouth Borough Police
(1836 - 1859)

Liskeard Borough Police
(1836 - 1877)

Okehampton Borough Police
(1836 - 1860)

Penryn Borough Police
(1836 - 1889)

South Molton Borough Police
(1836 - 1877)

Penzance Borough Police
(1836 - 1947)

Tavistock Borough Police
(1837 - 1856)

St. Ives Borough Police
(1836 - 1889)

Tiverton Borough Police
(1845 - 1943)

Truro City Police
(1836 - 1921)

Torrington Borough Police
(1836 - 1870) & (1878 - 1886)

Isles of Scilly Police
(1836 - 1947)

Totnes Borough Police
(1836 - 1884)

(Other borough forces, such as Torquay District, existed but little
documentary evidence remains of them. Also, many of the old
parish police forces were in use for many years until being taken
over by the larger forces detailed in this table)

Wolborough Borough Police
(1836 - 1859)

Introduction

Such a small volume cannot possibly hope to catalogue every aspect of policing which has occurred since the advent of photography over 150 years ago, nor can it dare to assume to be a definitive history of policing in this south western peninsula of England. It can, however, justifiably be regarded as a simple tribute to policing and a lasting memorial to our constabulary forefathers to whom we, in the police service of today, owe a debt of immeasurable gratitude. It is to those officers of yesteryear, who served in the many police forces which have evolved to become the Devon & Cornwall Constabulary, that we turn to seek approval in hoping that this record is a fitting acknowledgement of their efforts. Little known old forces like the Truro City Police, the Barnstaple Borough Police and the Isles of Scilly Police all developed, no doubt with a tinge of sentimentality from the more parochial officers, into larger forces - the Cornwall County, Plymouth and Exeter Cities and Devon County, to name but a few - and all played their role in forging the future of the police service throughout the South West.

Through these few pages it can be seen that despite the differences in uniforms and equipment, policing always has been, and still remains, a partnership between the police and the community we serve. Without society's support there would be a very much different police service present in our cities, towns and villages. Hopefully, the reader who browses through these pages will find something which brings a refreshing insight and understanding into the world of the police service; whether you are an historian looking at the uniforms with a critical eye, or just casually enjoying pictures of a bygone age.

There is never a shortage of good men and women who wish to proudly wear our uniform. The Devon & Cornwall Constabulary has justifiably earned a reputation within the police service nationally which continues to attract applicants and transfer requests from all over the country. This book, hopefully, captures all that is good in a service which is built upon a foundation of co-operation and trust. Ours is a service in the Westcountry which prides itself in the expression *Community Policing*, first used in the 1970s to describe our own inimitable style, and which other forces still strive to emulate.

Simon Dell, MBE
Police Constable 1191
1st January 2000

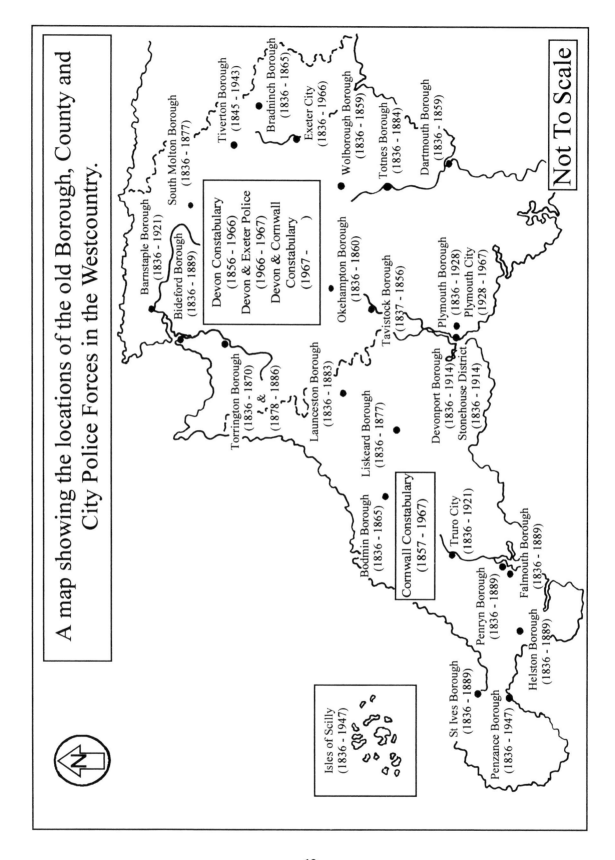

A map showing the locations of the old Borough, County and City Police Forces in the Westcountry.

Not To Scale

N

Barnstaple Borough
(1836 - 1921)

South Molton Borough
(1836 - 1877)

Tiverton Borough
(1845 - 1943)

Bradninch Borough
(1836 - 1865)

Exeter City
(1836 - 1966)

Wolborough Borough
(1836 - 1859)

Totnes Borough
(1836 - 1884)

Dartmouth Borough
(1836 - 1859)

Bideford Borough
(1836 - 1889)

Devon Constabulary
(1856 - 1966)
Devon & Exeter Police
(1966 - 1967)
Devon & Cornwall
Constabulary
(1967 -   )

Okehampton Borough
(1836 - 1860)

Tavistock Borough
(1837 - 1856)

Plymouth Borough
(1836 - 1928)
Plymouth City
(1928 - 1967)

Torrington Borough
(1836 - 1870)
&
(1878 - 1886)

Launceston Borough
(1836 - 1883)

Liskeard Borough
(1836 - 1877)

Devonport Borough
(1836 - 1914)
Stonehouse District
(1836 - 1914)

Bodmin Borough
(1836 - 1865)

Cornwall Constabulary
(1857 - 1967)

Truro City
(1836 - 1921)

Falmouth Borough
(1836 - 1889)

Penryn Borough
(1836 - 1889)

St Ives Borough
(1836 - 1889)

Helston Borough
(1836 - 1889)

Penzance Borough
(1836 - 1947)

Isles of Scilly
(1836 - 1947)

The Era of the Parish Constable

The commencement of commercial photography coincided with the time of the introduction of police forces. Therefore, few photographs exist of the days of the locally-appointed parish constables; those which do have been taken from either glass plate negatives or old documents and artefacts such as in these examples.

Right. George Gater Potter. The last recorded parish constable of Abbotskerswell, a village near the town of Newton Abbot. This photographic print was taken from an old glass plate negative dated about 1860, or possibly a little earlier, at a time of the infancy of the Devon Constabulary.

He is pictured here with his wife, who, like many women of that age, emulated the style of dress of Queen Victoria, at that time in mourning for her late husband, Prince Albert.

(Mrs Frances Peek)

Below. The parish vestry record of Lamerton Parish, near Tavistock, of 1st April 1852, detailing the appointment of the eight local parish constables for the year. The records were so-called because the meetings of this parish committee took place in the vestry of the parish church.

List of Persons Qualified and Liable, and duly Nominated by a Vestry, to Serve as Constables for the Parish of *Lamerton* in the Division of Tavistock, in the County of Devon, for the year 1852

CHRISTIAN AND SURNAME.	PLACE OF ABODE.	TITLE, QUALITY, CALLING, OR BUSINESS.
John Percy	Lamerton	Registrar
William Brook	Whitslade	Yeoman
William Percy	Headwell	Yeoman
Arthur Stanbury	Woodly	Yeoman
Samuel Palmer	Trevenn	Yeoman
William Rice	North Brentor	Blacksmith
William Cook	South Brentor	Yeoman
John Williams	Woodmanswell	Yeoman

NOTICE.—All objections to the foregoing List will be heard by Her Majesty's Justices of the Peace, acting for the said Division, at the Guildhall, in Tavistock, on Thursday First day of April 1852, at Eleven o'clock in the fore noon.

Overseers of the Poor of the Parish of Lamerton

Overseers' Return of Constables.—Printed ?, S. CHAVE, Tavistock.

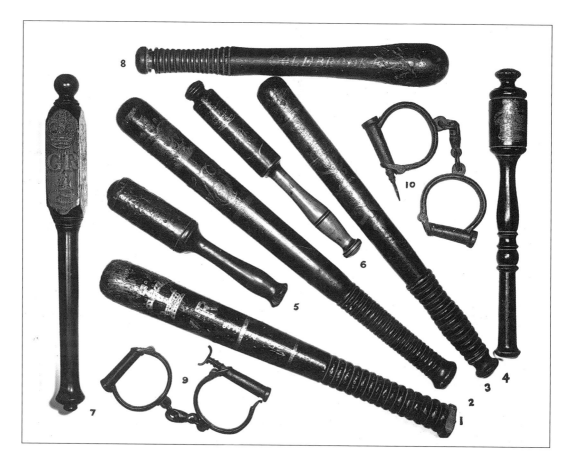

Part of the collection of parish constables' truncheons, tipstaffs and handcuffs held by former Chief Inspector J. Luscombe of the Devon Constabulary.

1. Parish constable's truncheon from East Allington.   2. Parish constable's truncheon from Stoke Fleming.
3. Parish constable's truncheon from Bere Ferrers.   4. Parish constable's truncheon from Peter Tavy.
5. Parish constable's tipstaff from Ugborough dated 1819. 6. Parish constable's tipstaff from Meavy 1832.
7. Parish constable's truncheon from Diptford 1822.   8. Parish constable's truncheon from Colebrook.
9 and 10. Handcuffs from the same period.

The parish constable's tipstaff and, later, truncheon were 'badges of office' as opposed to their modern-day use as weapons of defence. These officers wore no uniforms, so many used to hang their truncheons outside their cottages so as to indicate their presence and authority. The 'office' of parish constable was often an unpopular one, for they received no wages and many attempted to buy their way out of having to serve.

The parish constable was elected once a year by the 'vestry' meeting in each parish. However, once the Devon Constabulary had been formed in 1856 the locally-appointed parish constables passed into policing history.

Transportation Warrant 1813. This warrant was issued at the 'General Quarter Sessions of the Peace' in the borough of Plympton Earle and relates to the conviction of Robert Bartlett who stole one pick, one sledge, one hook and one iron hatchet, the property of Robert Marshall. Bartlett was convicted and sentenced to be "Transported beyond the seas" for a period of seven years, and the parish constable of Plympton placed him in the borough gaol before taking him to Portsmouth for the voyage.

£5. REWARD!

WHEREAS,

On the Evening of SUNDAY, 24th. of December Inst.;

During the time the Family were at Chapel, the House of Mr. J. MILWARD, of East-Street, NEWTON-ABBOT, was entered, and the following Property was Stolen therefrom; viz.—

"6 Silver Table-Spoons, Marked "J. M." A Pair of Silver Sugar-Tongs, Marked "J. M." 2 Silver "Table-Spoons, not Marked. 12 Electro-plated Forks, not Marked. 1 Silver Cream Ladle, not Marked. "4 Silver Salt-Spoons, not Marked. 2 Silver Mugs, with a "STAG" impressed thereon. 1 Gold Ring, "Marked "J. S. M." containing Hair. 1 Bead Purse, containing £1:9:6."

The above Reward will be given to any Person, or Persons, who shall give such Information as shall lead to the Apprehension, Conviction, and Recovery of the said Property.

Information to be given to

Mr. W. T. BAKER,
Superintendent of Police, Newton-Abbot.

Dated, December 25th., 1854.

Sluman, Printer, &c,; East-Street, Newton-Abbot.

A 'Reward' poster dated 25th December 1854, some two years prior to the formation of the Devon Constabulary. The superintendent of police, Mr. W. T. Baker, would, in fact, have been the head constable for the parish of Newton Abbot. Many head constables were known as superintendents, and upon amalgamation with the new county force in 1856 most were offered positions as sergeants in the Devon Constabulary.

Isles of Scilly Police
(1836 - 1947)

It was in 1942 that Sergeant Wherry and Constable Hobbs of the Cornwall Constabulary were sent to the Isles of Scilly to reinforce the local St. Mary's parish police officer during the war years; it wasn't until 1947 that the responsibility for policing the islands fell to the Cornwall Constabulary. Until that time, the island authorities appointed their own uniformed officer who policed this furthest part of the south western peninsula in much the same way as his parish constable forebears. Following the 1947 amalgamation the formal name of the new force was the 'Cornwall and Isles of Scilly Constabulary', although this title was rarely used. From that time the old parish constable system used on the islands ceased and only Cornwall Constabulary men served there, usually for periods of two years at a time.

Constable Horatio Nelson, 1865.

Constable Horatio Nelson was the second paid officer for the parish of St. Mary's, covering all the various islands. The first paid officer was James Hicks. Horatio was appointed in 1865, but finally dismissed in 1875 following numerous complaints made about him. It was decided by the island authorities to replace him with another officer "with less profane and intemperate language and better moral conduct". His tombstone can be found in the Old Town Churchyard, a few yards to the south-east of the church.

(Isles of Scilly Museum)

Above. Cornwall Constabulary Constables Ernie Reynolds and Peter Ward were the only two 'regular' officers on the islands, stationed at St. Mary's. It was not until the 1960s that the complement became one sergeant and a constable.

(Mrs B. James)

Above. The Isles of Scilly, Cornwall Constabulary officers photographed in February 1959 at the rear of the old police station on St. Mary's. Standing, left to right: Constable Ernie Reynolds, Special Constable N. J. (Johnny) James and Constable Peter Ward.
Seated: Special Constables George Nicholls and Jack Williams.

(Mrs B. James)

Above. A visit to St. Mary's by the Queen Mother in about 1968, with Constable Frederick White to the fore. Although this was taken after the 1967 formation of the Devon & Cornwall Constabulary, Constable White is still wearing the Cornwall Constabulary uniform as he was posted to the islands when they were still policed by the Cornwall force.

(Josephine Shadrick)

Left. Constable Des Bird with the school-children of Carn Warvel School, on St. Mary's, presenting their cycle proficiency certificates in September 1979. Also present at the ceremony is the chairman of the council (as well as an Isles of Scilly member of the Devon & Cornwall Constabulary Police Authority), Councillor Sam Ellis.

A few years later, when Constable Bird was promoted, he returned to St. Mary's as a sergeant to continue his love of policing these islands as the officer in charge.

(Mrs B. James)

Right. Sergeant Bill Newton in 1981, pictured outside the islands' police station. The usual complement of the island force is just one sergeant and one constable, both officers living in houses above the police station. This is often supplemented, in the summer months, by another unmarried officer from the 'Cornwall Area', who lives in the flat attached to the police station. The official transport supplied for patrol duties and policing the main island, St. Mary's, is now invariably a Landrover.
(Mr W. Newton)

Left. Sergeant Bill Newton, his constable and Sergeant Peter Phillips (centre) on St. Mary's quayside in about 1981. It was Sergeant Phillips, from Headquarters, who conducted the boat authorisation tests for officers stationed on the islands for many years.

The island officers probably did more mileage in their small boat than in their land vehicle as during the course of their duties they had to visit and patrol all the inhabited islands. A boat, therefore, was (and still is) an essential part of policing there.

(Mr W. Newton)

Right. Special Constable 'Johnny' James pictured at his retirement presentation on St. Mary's with the Chief Constable of the Devon & Cornwall force, Donald Elliott, and Chief Superintendent John Allen, the Divisional Commander of the West Cornwall Division. 'Johnny' had served 30 continuous years on the islands.

Johnny's wife, Barbara, became a special constable in 1981, and served for 17 years herself.

(Mrs B. James)

Left. Another photograph taken on the occasion of the retirement of Special Constable James.

Those pictured are, left to right: Woman Special Constable Barbara James, Special Constable 'Johnny' James, Sergeant Mike Brookes, Chief Superintendent John Allen, Her Majesty's Inspector of Constabulary Mr Brian Weight, Chief Constable Donald Elliott, Constable Pat Martin, Special Constable Gary Hoyle and a recent, but unnamed, applicant to the Special Constabulary.

(Mrs B. James)

Right. In more recent times transport for officers on St. Mary's has usually been a Landrover, seen here with the island of Tresco in the background. The local constable's job may seem idyllic when compared to that of his inner city colleagues, but should he face disorder or other such problems caused in the busy summer months, his nearest support from other duty officers could be some hours away.

CORNWALL COUNTY
Penzance Borough Police
(1836 - 1947)

This small borough force was formed in 1836, along with many other borough forces in the country, following the 'Municipal Corporation Act' of 1835, which required every borough to appoint a 'Watch Committee' with a duty of maintaining a police force. The officers were housed in the basement of St. John's Hall with their Chief Constable, and this remained the pattern until the force was eventually amalgamated into the Cornwall Constabulary. Nationally, in an effort to reduce the number of police forces with which the military authorities had to deal during the Second World War, the Home Office amalgamated certain of the smaller borough police forces with the local county force. Therefore, in 1943, Penzance Borough temporarily went over to the county constabulary until the 1946 'Police Act', which abolished non-county borough police forces such as Penzance. As a result, from 1947 the town was policed solely by the Cornwall Constabulary and Penzance became the last of the old borough forces in the Westcountry to be taken over.

Penzance Borough Police, seen here in 1914 outside St. John's Hall. To the left is the chairman of the 'Watch Committee', the forerunner to the modern-day police authority.

RULES AND REGULATIONS

FOR THE

TREATMENT AND CONDUCT OF PRISONERS

IN THE GAOL AND HOUSE OF CORRECTION,

IN THE BOROUGH OF PENZANCE,

Pursuant to Act of Parliament, 4, Geo. 4, Cap. 64.

1st. ALL Prisoners, when brought into the Prison, shall be examined by the Surgeon previous to being passed into their respective Cells, and shall be cleansed in a warm or cold Bath; but Prisoners before trial, or Misdemeanants of the First Division, shall be bathed and cleansed only when absolutely necessary for health and cleanliness, provided always that no Prisoner shall be stripped and bathed in the presence of any other Prisoner. Prisoners after conviction, &c., shall be clothed in the Prison Dress, and, in order to preserve cleanliness, their hair shall be cut and kept short.

2nd. ALL money, watches, and other valuable property, as well as all knives and other articles likely to facilitate escape, shall be taken from them and delivered into the charge of the Deputy Gaoler, who shall immediately enter the particulars thereof into a book kept for that purpose;—all such articles to be returned to the owners at their discharge, or to such other person on his or her behalf as may be directed by the Visiting Justices, and the Prisoners shall sign the book as an acknowledgment of their property having been so restored.

3rd. PRISONERS when discharged, who have not any money, and who have behaved well during their imprisonment, may be allowed a small sum at their discharge, at the discretion of the Mayor.

4th. No Prisoner who is confined under the sentence of any Court, nor any Prisoner confined in pursuance of any Conviction before a Justice, shall receive any food, clothing, or necessaries, other than the Gaol allowance, except Prisoners convicted of Misdemeanors of the First Division.

5th. THE established Dietary for Prisoners maintained at the expence of the Borough shall in no case be departed from, nor shall any Wine, Spirits, Beer, or other Liquor be admitted for the use of any Prisoner, except under the special directions of the Mayor or one or more of the Visiting Justices, or of the Surgeon in case of sickness:—except in the case of Prisoners before trial, who may be allowed to provide for themselves Malt Liquor not exceeding one pint in the twenty-four hours, and in the case of convicted Misdemeanants of the First Division.

6th. PRISONERS confined for any supposed offence shall before trial be permitted to receive, at proper times, such food, clothing, or other necessaries as may be consistent with the discipline of the Prison, and subject to strict examination by the Deputy Gaoler.

7th. PRISONERS sentenced to Hard Labour at the Tread Wheel or other work shall be allowed an extra quantity of Bread (not exceeding a half a pound), at the discretion of the Deputy Gaoler.

8th. ALL Letters, written by or sent to any Prisoner, except such as are addressed to the Secretary of State, the Visiting Justices, or other proper authorities, shall be inspected by the Governor and Chaplain, and in every instance in which either of them shall deem it expedient to withhold a letter, either to or from any Prisoner, the Governor shall lay every such letter before a Visiting Justice for his decision. But nothing in this Rule shall extend to impede the communications of Prisoners committed for trial with their friends or legal adviser; and such Prisoners, as well as all others, will be allowed Pens, Ink, and Paper, at the discretion of the Deputy Gaoler.

9th. PRISONERS committed for Trial shall be permitted to see their friends, legal adviser, and other persons necessary for their defence, at proper times and under proper restrictions; and all other Prisoners shall be allowed to see their friends at the discretion of the Mayor or his Deputy.

10th. EVERY Officer is strictly forbidden to strike any Prisoner, or to use any violent or abusive language: but, in all cases of misconduct on the part of the Prisoners, he is to report the same forthwith to the Mayor.

11th. ALL Prisoners shall obey the lawful orders of the Deputy Gaoler for rising, meal time, work, and bed time, which shall be as follow. The Hours of Rising shall be regulated as follow:—a warning bell shall be rung in the Prison at Half-past Five o'Clock in the Morning from the First of April to the First of September, both inclusive, and at Half an Hour before

Sun-rising at all other times in the year, on the ringing of which bell all Prisoners shall rise, dress themselves, sweep out their cells, and make their beds; another bell shall be rung at a Quarter of an Hour before Six o'Clock during the above-mentioned period, and at a Quarter of an Hour before Sun-rising at all other times of the year, when the Prisoners' cell doors shall be opened and they shall be called down to their courts to wash at the pumps (with the exception of such Prisoners as may have been ordered to remain confined to their cells for the whole or any part of the day, to whom water shall be supplied to wash themselves), and the cleanliness of the Prisoners, and the good order of their cells, shall be then inspected by the Deputy Gaoler. All Prisoners shall be locked up in their cells as soon as may be after Sun-setting throughout the year.

12th. ANY Prisoner, on application to the Deputy Gaoler, may be allowed an interview with the Chaplain of the Prison, and any Prisoner of a religious pursuation differing from that of the Established Church may, at the special request of such Prisoner, be visited by a Minister of such pursuation, duly licensed, at proper and reasonable times.

13th. THE Hours of Work shall be as follow:—from Sun-rising till Sun-setting during the months of November, December, January, and February, and from Six in the Morning till Half-past Five in the Evening the remainder of the year, deducting from such time the time allowed for meals. That every cell be provided with a Bible and Prayer Book.

THE DEPUTY GAOLER.

1st. THE Deputy Gaoler shall not take or receive to his own use any fee, gratuity, or emolument from or on account of any Prisoners committed to his custody.

2nd. HE shall execute his duties in person—he shall attend the Prisoners at the distribution of bread and other provisions—he shall superintend the supplies of the Prison and see that there is no defraud—he shall enter all accounts and receipts of supplies in a book to be kept for that purpose, and shall deliver in such accounts with the vouchers to the Mayor and Police Committee the first Thursday in every month.

3rd. HE shall keep a Journal or Book, in which he shall enter a list of all Prisoners, as well as all Clothing or other Property deposited in his hands, and to be preserved by him until their discharge.

4th. HE shall see that all rules relating to the internal regulation and discipline of the Prison be duly and strictly enforced.

THE MATRON.

1st. THE Matron shall consider herself as responsible to the Deputy Gaoler, receive directions from him from time to time, and she shall be the only person allowed to search the Female Prisoners, or Female Visitors.

2nd. In the event of sickness, or unavoidable absence, the Deputy Gaoler may appoint a Female, not a Prisoner, to act as an Assistant, subject to the approval of the Mayor.

THE SURGEON.

1st. THE Surgeon shall be appointed annually by the Mayor and shall visit the Prison once every day, and immediately on a notice from the Deputy Gaoler that any Prisoner is ill. He shall, after such visit, enter in his journal any circumstance respecting the state of body or mind of any Prisoner who may require immediate attention, or any alteration in diet or discipline which he may think necessary, or when any extra bedding, clothing, food, or liquors, necessary for the use of any Prisoner, and such entry shall be sufficient authority to the Deputy Gaoler to procure the same.

2nd. HE shall report to the Deputy Gaoler all cases where an attempt has been made to impose on him by pretended indisposition, and the same shall be communicated to the Mayor and investigated, and if proved the offender shall be punished according to the circumstances of the offence.

THE PRISONERS

Are strictly enjoined to attend to the following Rules for regulating their own conduct, any violation of which, as well as any other act of misconduct or disobedience not herein specified, will be punished as the Law authorizes:—

1st. WHENEVER any Magistrate, stranger, or Officer of the Prison enters the Prison yard you are to be respectful in your behaviour—you are to use civility to the Deputy Gaoler, and obey all his lawful directions — you are to be clean in your persons and peaceable and orderly in your whole conduct and demeanor.

2nd. You are not to play at dice, cards, or any other kind of gaming whatever — you are not to fight or wrestle, or use abusive or profane language of any kind.

3rd. You are not to exact from your fellow Prisoners any money or other thing under the name of garnish, or any other pretence, nor are you to cobb or otherwise illtreat them.

4th. You are to observe strict silence whilst at labour and when locked up in your respective sleeping cells, and you are not to make any unnecessary noise.

5th. You are not to destroy or injure any articles, either of clothing or other necessaries, belonging to the Borough, nor are you to write on or otherwise deface or damage the wall or any other part of the Prison whatever.

6th. You are not to boil water in your tin pots, nor to cook in any way whatever by the fires in your respective rooms, nor are you, if under charge of or conviction of any crime, to smoke or use tobacco or snuff in any way whatever.

THE DIETARY ALLOWED TO THE PRISONERS IN THE PENZANCE GAOL.

			BREAKFAST.	DINNER.	SUPPER.
SUNDAY	Bread, 1½ lb		Gruel, 1 Pint	Meat, 5 oz.	Gruel, 1 Pint.
MONDAY	Ditto		Ditto	Potatoes, 1½ lb	Ditto.
TUESDAY	Ditto		Ditto	Soup, 1 Pint	Ditto.
WEDNESDAY	Ditto		Ditto	Potatoes, 1½ lb	Ditto.
THURSDAY	Ditto		Ditto	Meat, 5 oz.	Ditto.
FRIDAY	Ditto		Ditto	Potatoes, 1½ lb	Ditto.
SATURDAY	Ditto		Ditto	Soup, 1 Pint	Ditto.

WHITEHALL, 5th September, 1840.

The annexed Rules and Regulations, for the Government of the Gaol and House of Correction for the Borough of Penzance, having been submitted to me, I hereby certify that they are proper to be enforced.

NORMANBY.

Above. Taken in about 1936, this photograph shows, from left to right, rear row: Constables Symonds, Eddy, Cutler, Beer, Radford and Richards; middle row: Brown, Hancock, Davis, unknown, Fowler, Lock and Bartlett; front row: Constable Chegwidden, Sergeants Curnow and Matthews, Chief Constable Kenyon, Sergeant Webber and Constables Carne and Fulford.

(Mrs Mary Rogers)

Above. The Penzance force pictured in about 1939 with its new Chief Constable, Mr Robert Jenkins. Note the change in the helmet plate badges from chrome to black and chrome.

Penzance Borough Police, July 1939.

Included in the photograph are: (back row) Constables 7 Jackson and 3 Tapping; (third row) Constables 18 Hicks, 16 Botheras, 14 Green, 17 Adamson, 15 Toms, 12 Eddy and 11 Cutler; (second row) Constables 4 Ferris, 5 Davis, 10 Beer, 13 Symons, 6 Hancock, 9 Radford, 8 Richards and 2 Lock; (front row) Sergeants 5 Brown, 3 Bartlett, 1 Curnow, Cllr. F. S. Shaw (Chairman of the Watch Committee), R. C. M. Jenkins (Chief Constable), Cllr. J. Birch J.P. (Mayor), Sergeants 2 Fulford and 4 Fowler and Constable 1 Chegwidden. (Upon promotion to sergeant, the constables had their collar numbers changed accordingly.)

Penzance Borough Police, 1941. During the war years the police were supported, as always, by the volunteers of the 'Special Constabulary', who had the letters 'SC' on their collars. Like many other police forces, extra 'War Reserve' officers were recruited. These were generally former policemen brought out of retirement and who had 'WR' on their collars. The cap badges of the Special Constabulary can be seen as small crowns, as opposed to the larger star badges of the war reserve officers.

Above. Helmet plate prior to 1938. The insignia of the head of St. John the Baptist on a plate was worn by the force in recognition of their station being in St. John's Hall in the town.

(Jeff Cowdell)

Above. The belt buckle also showed the insignia of the head of St. John the Baptist on a plate. This was also repeated on the buttons. The star shaped cap badge shows the borough crest.

(Dave Wilkinson)

Left. Helmet plate after 1938. After about 1938 the insignia of St. John the Baptist's head on badges and buttons was changed in favour of the borough crest. This style of helmet plate and insignia then remained with the force until its amalgamation into the Cornwall Constabulary a few years later. Several other forces, nationally, at about this time were developing their insignia to reflect coats of arms and crests, which were eventually replaced by the standard 'royal cipher'. At the same time, however, many officers in the small and parochial forces saw these small, but significant, changes as detrimental steps, moving away from their individual character and identity.

(Jeff Cowdell)

Truro City Police
(1836 - 1921)

Like many other police forces, Truro started life as a 'borough' police force, but changed its name in the late 19th century to Truro City Police so as to reflect its status as a police force in this 'Cathedral City'. When this small city force amalgamated with the Cornwall Constabulary on 1st March 1921, the Home Office approved an increase in the manpower of the Cornwall Constabulary of two sergeants and ten constables.

Truro Borough Police, 1870. Seen here with their senior officer, Superintendent Woodcock, are, from left to right, Sergeant Roberts and Constables Coad, Collett, Scown and Bettison.

(Jeff Cowdell)

Truro City Police, 1890. Having changed its name from a borough force, Truro also underwent a change of uniform to reflect its 'new' status. At the same time, the rank of the senior officer also changed from superintendent to Chief Constable. Seen here with the force's Chief Constable, Mr Angel, Truro was distinguished somewhat by being one of only a few in the Westcountry ever to use the 'Metropolitan Police' style 'duty band': officers would be obliged to wear their uniforms at all times and the duty band was removed when 'off duty'. Sergeants also took to wearing the conventional chevrons on the arms of their tunics, although the helmet plate badges for sergeants were chrome as opposed to black for constables.

(Jeff Cowdell)

Right. Truro City Sergeant 1.
Once promoted, the constables
changed their 'collar numbers' to new
ones in order to reflect their new rank.
The crest of the city police is shown
on the collar as well as on the chrome
helmet plate badge. This photograph,
which has been touched-in with
watercolour paint, would have been
taken in about 1910. Those with an
eye for detail will note that the whistle
chain is leading to the right breast
pocket as opposed to the left, as in the
majority of forces. Also, the chain
enters the pocket on the outside edge
of the button, which is most
uncommon. The familiar large circular
St. John's First Aid badge was also
worn above the chevrons, as was often
found in many police forces of the
day.

Left. A Victorian helmet plate
badge as worn by a constable
of the Truro City Police circa
1880. This badge would have
been used prior to the crest
being displayed, as in the 1890
photograph on the previous
page.

(Vic Denyer)

Right. A constable's helmet
plate badge of the early 1920s,
showing the crest and a king's
crown. This was the final badge
used by constables of the force.

(Metropolitan Police Museum)

Truro City Police, 1921. The last photograph taken of this force just prior to its amalgamation with the Cornwall County Constabulary on 1st March 1921. The Chief Constable, Mr Angel, had been the senior officer for over 30 years, for it is he, as a much younger man, who appears in the 1890 photograph of the force, as seen previously on page 28.

The officers' whistle chains are still being worn in an unusual manner whereby they are to the right and to the outside of the pocket button. Such small peculiarities vanished along with this small city force, although several of the old 'Truro City' men went on to serve in the Cornwall force for many more years, not being required to leave the city to serve elsewhere in the county in deference to their old force.

Launceston Borough Police
(1836 - 1883)

This important and historic town, known as the 'Gateway to Cornwall', had its own borough force from the earliest opportunity, but it consisted of only one officer: although the Cornwall County Constabulary policed the rural area known as the 'Launceston division', the county superintendent had his office at Camelford. When the Launceston Borough Police was taken over by the Cornwall Constabulary in 1883, however, the superintendent's office was moved to Launceston.

Left. A helmet plate badge of the Launceston Police, but thought to be that of Launceston city in Tasmania and not the town in Cornwall.

Right. **Edward Barrett,** the only full-time constable of Launceston Borough, from 1860 to 1883, was a Cornishman, born at St. Mellion, near Saltash, and only retired upon the amalgamation of the Launceston Borough into the county force in 1883.

(Launceston Museum)

St. Ives Borough Police
(1836 - 1889)

Formed like many others in 1836, this police force only ever consisted of one officer at any time, known as the 'Head Constable', and he had two cells in the town hall basement. The Inspector of Constabulary's report of 29th September, 1876 greatly criticised the St. Ives Borough, along with many other similar borough forces in the county, as being "too small and inefficient to be worthy of keeping." St. Ives, however, held out until 1889, when pressure to amalgamate with the Cornwall Constabulary, which subsequently took over the policing of the town, became too great.

Right. A St. Ives Borough officer dated about 1854. His uniform was similar to many borough forces of that period, with frock coat and top hat. Many officers, incidentally, applied tar to their hats so as to make them waterproof.

The John Knill Ceremony, circa 1856. This has been held every five years with a procession through the town culminating at the monument erected by John Knill, one of the prominent personalities of the area. The St. Ives constable can be seen in top hat to the left of the monument, next to the fiddler, although this photograph is an excellent example of social history in its own right.

Cornwall Constabulary
(1857 - 1967)

Unlike the older borough police forces created in 1836 after the 'Municipal Corporation Act' of 1835, the Cornwall County Constabulary did not come about until 1857. Until that time it was felt that the borough forces and the locally-appointed parish constables in the rural areas could manage the general policing requirements of the county.

Once formed, the Cornwall Constabulary gradually took over the smaller borough and city forces, until it, too, became the subject of amalgamation when, in 1967, the Devon & Cornwall Constabulary was formed. Nevertheless, evidence of the old uniforms still being worn by many of the former Cornwall county officers remained for some years, since they were keen to retain a degree of pride and identity with the old county force.

Left. One of the first officers to serve in the new Cornwall Constabulary, seen here wearing the uniform of the day, which comprised a frock coat and top hat. The uniform at that time followed closely with the style of the uniform of the old borough forces which, in themselves, were often modelled on the old uniforms of the London police.

Right. The Redruth Borough stocks seen in about 1860. It is an interesting quirk of history to note that this method of punishment was never repealed by Act of Parliament, but its last recorded use in Great Britain was in about 1865, in Rugby, not long after this photograph was taken.

The officers are of the newly-formed Cornwall Constabulary, and are pictured outside their station in the town. From the expression on the faces of the officers, and indeed, that of the unfortunate young man, it might tend to suggest that the photograph could have been taken as a final, slightly tongue-in-cheek reminder of the use of the stocks, rather than a record of them being used 'in anger'.

The Royal Cornwall Show, circa 1859. The curly-brimmed style of helmet without any helmet plate badge was common in police forces of that time until they had established their own uniform identity. This group photograph of distinguished guests at the Royal Cornwall Show includes several Cornwall Constabulary officers in their distinctive, but short-lived helmets.

Above. St. Cleer Police Station, on the fringes of Bodmin Moor near Liskeard, was built in 1859 at the rear of the church. It had high ground-floor windows fortified by heavy shutters, which provided protection to the constable and his family who lived in the station during the violent clashes with militant Cornish miners.

Below. Sergeant Major George Piddick was appointed in 1857 at the very start of the Cornwall Constabulary. He is seen here on the lawn of Priory House at Bodmin teaching the young daughters of Colonel Gilbert, the Chief Constable, how to perform 'staff drill.'

MICHELL & SON · · S⸝ AUSTELL

Left. Cornwall County officer, circa 1878. This photograph shows the new style of helmet which replaced the top hat and which was being brought into use nationally as other police forces developed their uniform styles. It was based upon the military helmet of the day and, although many forces had slight variations, the general style was very similar.

Well over a century later this style of helmet, with a little variation, is still used in the county. The constable, however, is still wearing the old pattern tunic, which took a little longer to develop and change, with his number still on his collar alongside the Victorian crown. To this day, the officer's identification number, although now worn on the shoulder epaulette, is still referred to as a 'collar number'. This is a small throwback to our constabulary forebears, which many regard as an important aspect of tradition and individual identity of the police service.

Right. A Cornwall Constabulary officer, 1880. Following the introduction of the new type of helmet, the tunics for the Cornwall officers also altered a few years later. As can be seen in this photograph, the collar numbers and crown have been removed from the neck and relocated to the left breast. On this breast badge the officer's numbers and crown were embroidered on cloth which was sewn onto the tunic. Both the numbers and crown were in red on a black background. Not many police forces adopted this rather individual way in which to identify its officers, and indeed the Cornwall Constabulary did not use this style of badge for many years.

Upon joining the force, many officers had their photographs taken in this style of formal pose. The presence of the old stocks, whose use had not long since been discontinued, added a degree of formality and dignity to the occasion.

Above. The St. Columb horse-bus being used to transport a handcuffed prisoner to Bodmin gaol, circa 1880.

Below. Constable William Braund, and his family, outside the Landue Bridge police cottage, between Launceston and Callington, in about 1880. He died a few years later from pneumonia, caught whilst keeping observations for chicken thieves in the rain, at night.

(Len Maddever)

Camborne Riots, 19th April 1882. This photograph shows the officers who were sent as reinforcements to the Camborne area in order to quell the riotous miners. The disorder experienced by police officers in the 19th century, particularly in mining areas, was great indeed. The Riot Act was frequently read out by local magistrates, invoking powers upon the police to use great force if necessary to restore order. There are numerous accounts of severe injuries being inflicted on both sides during these frequent disturbances.

An early group photograph of Cornwall Constabulary officers taken in about 1885. The Cornish fashion of the day of having rather fulsome beards continued in the Cornwall Constabulary, while many other forces forbade officers to wear such facial adornments. Note the sergeants, who wore their chevrons on the right forearms of their tunics.

Above. The sergeant major, wearing his distinctive reversed chevrons and crown, with a class of recruits at Headquarters in Bodmin, circa 1895. This, however, was a short-lived rank and one not shared by many other forces.

Below. A group photograph taken in about 1898, the scene looking more like a casual picnic than a formal occasion.

"A CORNISH PASTY, I'M RUNNING 'IM IN," N°27

Above left. Superintendent W. H. Beare, the Deputy Chief Constable of Cornwall, on his horse at Headquarters, Bodmin in about 1900.

Above right. A rather cheeky postcard, dated around 1900, from a series of Cornish life pictures. This tramp was 'recruited' for the photograph, but care was obviously taken to hide the identity of the guilty officer: it can be seen that the red embroidered number and crown (which would surely have identified the culprit) have been carefully covered up with material!

(Dave Kierans)

Right. Sergeant Thomas Hall, and his wife, pictured here upon his promotion on 29th November 1891. By now sergeants wore their chevrons on their upper arms, but were still to have no numbers on their uniforms for many years. Sergeant Hall had joined the Cornwall force on 25th August 1865, but he had also served on attachment to several of the borough forces in Cornwall, namely Bodmin, Penzance, Helston and Truro. He retired on 4th May 1895, after 30 years service.

(Jeff Cowdell)

Cottage fire, circa 1897. Then, as now, police work had its fair share of tragedy. In this photograph a constable is pictured leaning on his cycle, in company with his sergeant, at the scene of a cottage fire. Its location is not known, but it was clearly a significant event in the village to warrant this fine picture being taken. With relatively primitive fire-fighting equipment in the 19th century, most cottage fires in villages resulted in the dwelling being totally destroyed before any help could arrive at the location.

The construction of Falmouth Police Station in 1901. Whilst showing no police officers of the day, this fine photograph of the labour-intensive workforce used to erect such buildings justifies its place in this volume (as well as being the author's first station). The late 19th and early 20th centuries saw a large building programme of stations in the county to replace old and unsuitable accommodation, occupied since the start of the constabulary. This fine building is no longer used as the police station, but its ornate granite frontage is now listed and rightly preserved.

Road Accident, circa 1904. The age of the motor car certainly brought with it added work for the local constabulary. Here, Inspector K. Miller of Wadebridge and Constable Pomery deal with a horse killed by a car at Halfway, St. Issey, near Wadebridge. The officers' cycles rest in the nearby hedge (**above**), while Constable Pomery rests in the back of the offending car (**below**). What Inspector Miller's more modern-day counterpart might make of cycling to an accident, let alone allowing his constable to take a 'nap' in the back of the involved vehicle, remains to be guessed at!

Left. A king's crown 'garter' type badge of the Cornwall Constabulary. The wording of 'County Constabulary' was favoured by many forces at this time. Many other helmet plate badges were plain in the centre, but this one shows the 15 bazants of Cornwall.

(Jeff Cowdell)

Right. A more modern version of the badge on the left, now showing the words 'Cornwall Constabulary'. As helmet plate badges developed, greater local identity was created.

(Jeff Cowdell)

Road Accident, circa 1909. This early road traffic accident on Bodmin Moor, near the village of Minions, clearly shows the increased dangers that the age of the new motor car brought.

45

Clay Strike, circa 1913. Pictured at St. Austell during the Clay Strike of 1913, the Cornwall Constabulary cyclist section was used to great effect as a mobile body of officers. The officer in the cape is Constable (later Inspector) Hoskin.

The clay strikes around the St. Austell area became the subject of the play, 'Stocker's Copper', with numerous other police forces sending officers to Cornwall in order to assist the hard-pressed local constabulary.

Above. Officers from the Glamorgan Constabulary, with their distinctive silver chin chains, who were drafted in to assist Cornwall officers at St. Austell in 1913. They had arrived with shields, having recently come from the riots at Tonypandy mine in Wales, which unfortunately inflamed the Cornish clay workers. A solitary Cornish constable stands with them.

Below. A group of Cornwall officers in about 1920, pictured at a South Wales mine pit head during industrial unrest, when they took their turn in repaying the Glamorgan Constabulary for its assistance some years previously at St. Austell.

Falmouth officers, circa 1920.

This well-constructed picture shows the superintendent outside Falmouth station with his two sergeants and constables. As can be seen, the sergeants still wore no collar numbers and only had their chevrons on their right arms. The circular badge on the arm, incidentally, was the St. John's First Aid badge which most police forces had on their uniforms at this time. (The old red embroidered cloth numbers and crown on the left breast had been dispensed with by the Cornwall force prior to the Great War in favour of returning to collar numbers. Instead of the original crown beside the number, however, the crest of Cornwall appears for the first time. In addition, the helmet plate badge has now changed to chrome, and the constables are wearing service chevrons.)

When officers joined and were in their probationary period they wore no chevrons on their left cuff, but as they gained more service they became third, second and first-class constables. The officer seated on the left is a first-class constable with three stripes on his cuff. As in the majority of forces, the whistle chain goes to the left breast pocket.

The medal ribbons of some of the younger officers are from the Great War, which had not long since ended. The more senior officers, on the other hand, may well not have been called up for service, therefore no ribbons are shown on their tunics.

The ornate iron railings and illuminated sign over the front door were removed during the 1939-1945 war for smelting.

(Ret'd Superintendent C.D.Phillips
Gloucester Constabulary)

Above. Motorcycle officer, circa 1934. One of the first motorcycle patrol officers is seen here on a Sunbeam Lion motorcycle at Red Post, near Bude.

Above. Cornwall's first police car - an Austin 10 with 'dickie-seat' at the rear. Taken in the vicinity of a road accident near Bodmin Asylum in September 1936, the photograph also shows Inspector Sloman (on the right), Constable 99 Albert Clark - Cornwall's first motor patrol officer - and, in the helmet, Constable Rodney Thomas.

(Charles. L. Clark)

Above. The Traffic Division, seen here in about 1940, at the rear of its Bodmin Headquarters. The car on the left, ERL500, is the Chief Constable's and the officer stood alongside it is his chauffeur.

Above. Constable Tom Fox of Newquay on his Sunbeam motorcycle, photographed in about 1939.

Left. Constable 54 Harold Ollerearnshaw, wearing the new star type helmet plate, directing traffic in Truro city, in 1950.

(Harold Ollerearnshaw)

Above left and right. The new 'star' pattern of helmet plate badge was adopted by the Cornwall Constabulary after the 1939-1945 war, although in these examples the 15 bazants of Cornwall still appear with the king's crown. The slight differences in the wording, while seemingly insignificant, are nevertheless important to those in organisations such as the Police Insignia Collectors Association, who collect the thousands of helmet plate badges of forces throughout the country.

(Jeff Cowdell)

The Judge's Escort. The Assize Court (later to become the Crown Court) was held at Bodmin, and its judges were entitled to have officers escort them from the nearby parish church across to the court. These escorting officers, with their distinctive staffs, were known as 'Javelin men' and were under the command of a sergeant. Seen here in about 1950, this tradition existed for many years.

Above. PC 300 Doug Powell at the scene of a road accident at Red Post, near Bude in 1954. The high neck tunics were still being worn well into the 1950s by the Cornwall force.

(Doug Powell)

Below. The scene of the rescue of a dog which had fallen down cliffs near Bude in April 1956. Sergeant Horace Rees supervises hauling up Constable Frederick White who recovered the dog and received the R.S.P.C.A. medal and Queen's Commendation for his actions.

(Josephine Shadrick)

Above. The hard winter of 1958 on the A30 trunk road at Launceston. Sergeant Richards pauses by a stranded lorry whilst trying to clear the blocked main road.

(Charles Richards)

Below. Chief Inspector 'Jan' Deacon gives instruction to two constables on the new portable wireless system in about 1960.

Above. The radio control room at Bodmin Headquarters in about 1960, with PC Stothers. On his left can be seen the 'collators card' index system used to store records of known criminals - a far cry from today's modern communications centres and computer systems.

Above. Constable Frederick White of Bude poses in about 1963 with a young holidaymaker on the Strand in Bude.

(Josephine Shadrick)

Above. Constable White, proving to the amazement of some holidaymakers that Cornish policemen even have time to see ducks across the road!

(Josephine Shadrick)

Above. The queen's crown helmet plate and crests of the last officers to proudly wear the Cornwall Constabulary uniform. Upon amalgamation into the Devon & Cornwall Constabulary, the officers of the old Cornwall force had their shoulder numbers changed by adding about 1,620 to their existing old Cornish number so as to avoid duplication with officers of the Devon & Exeter Police.

(Dave Wilkinson)

Above. Woman Sergeant Liz Adcock and Woman Constable Ann Hobbs of the Policewomen's Department, outside Camborne Police Station in about 1961. Sergeant Adcock was later promoted to inspector and Constable Hobbs became Constable Moyle upon marriage.

Below. Constable 290 Edwards, seen in about 1963 in the force control room at Bodmin Headquarters, operating the telex machine - the terror of many officers with poor typing ability!

Below. Police cadets being taught to ride at Headquarters in Bodmin in about 1964.

THE BENNEY CONNECTION
FOUR GENERATIONS OF POLICING

Throughout the story of policing in the Westcountry there are many instances of son following in his father's footsteps by joining the force. There are one or two instances of even grandson following father and grandfather into the constabulary, but the generations of the Benney family must surely hold the record for service. Not only is there still a member of this Cornish family serving in the county, and not only did he follow his father, grandfather and great-grandfather into the force, but all four generations of these policemen have served in the same coastal village of St. Agnes, near Truro, at various times since 1896! Throughout the researching of this book, such a unique claim is unequalled anywhere, and probably unlikely to be repeated.

Below. Richard Henry Benney. Pictured here eating limpets at a St. Agnes 'chapel tea treat', Richard was appointed Constable 77 on 2nd February 1891 - after leaving his former employment as a miner. Following a short spell at Bodmin, and then Truro, he was posted to St. Agnes, where he remained for the rest of his service. In his service record it is recorded that he displayed "zeal, promptitude and intelligence" in the successful prosecution of a child murderer in 1901. He retired in 1919 with twenty-eight years total service, twenty-three of which were at St. Agnes.

Below. John Percival Benney. Seen here in the mid-1950s, 'Percy' (Richard's son and the officer at the rear wearing spectacles) was born at St. Agnes in 1899 and later worked at Barkla Shop on a grocery round before becoming a special constable in 1941. Soon afterwards he served as a police war reserve officer, enforcing air raid precautions and carrying out other wartime duties, but after the war he became a special constable again and assisted the St. Agnes officer until retiring in 1960.

Right. Kenneth Henry Benney. The son of 'Percy', Kenneth joined the Special Constabulary upon his father's retirement in 1960.

As a special constable in the 1960s his duties included attending a variety of carnivals and Flora Dances. He received his long service and good conduct medal in 1969 and retired in 1973.

This picture shows Kenneth with his daughter, Susan, taken just prior to a St. Agnes carnival in the 1960s. Kenneth was going on duty and Susan was an entrant in the carnival dressed as a 'Spanish lady'.

Below. Clive Benney, Community Constable, 1989. Kenneth's son, Clive, joined the Devon & Cornwall Constabulary as a cadet, four years after the amalgamation of the old Cornwall force, and became a constable in 1973. After first serving in Plymouth city and then in Camborne on motor patrol, he was posted to Perranporth in 1985 as a community beat officer for the St. Agnes and Perranporth areas, thus continuing this family tradition working the St. Agnes area, as his father, grandfather and great-grandfather had done before him.

Later, in 1990, Clive was promoted to sergeant, and is now a Traffic supervisor based at the Camborne Traffic Centre, retaining responsibilities for the St. Agnes area.

Apart from his police career, Clive is also an accomplished and well-regarded author on local history. In fact, in 1995 he was made a Cornish Bard for his work in the field of local history: his bardic name 'Gwythyas Sen Agnes Coth', means 'Guardian of Old St. Agnes'.

Author's note

Many thanks are due to Sergeant Clive Benney for supplying these photographs of his family, and for all the information upon which this section is based.

Above. An Identity Parade being held at Penzance in about 1965, in conditions which might seem rather primitive compared to today's two-way mirrors and video taping.

Below. The Final Parade. On 12th March 1967, in driving rain, the officers of the Cornwall Constabulary took part in a parade through the streets of the cathedral city of Truro to mark the end of 110 years of service to the county.

Pictured in the front is Arthur Pill, the Assistant Chief Constable of the Cornwall Constabulary, which was about to pass into history.

THE CITY OF PLYMOUTH
Devonport Borough Police
(1836 - 1914)

Although plans had been discussed as long ago as 1809 to form the 'Plymouth Dock Police' for this area of Plymouth (then known as 'Dock'), it was not until the 'Municipal Corporation Act' of 1835 that the Devonport Borough Police was formed. At the time this was a major undertaking because, due to Devonport having the status of a county borough, a substantial force had to be established, which, no doubt, quickly became well employed in this busy naval and shipbuilding port. However, with the advent of the Great War in 1914, together with the expansion of Plymouth as a city, the Devonport Borough Police amalgamated with the neighbouring Plymouth Borough force.

At this point it is worth mentioning that nearby Stonehouse, which had recently become the Divisional Headquarters of the Devon Constabulary's 'H' division, also had its own district police up until 1914, but that, too, was then taken over by the Plymouth Borough force. Meanwhile, the well-known naval expression of the day "as big as a Stonehouse policeman" bore some credibility, for only the toughest of men were recruited into this burly force whose main priority was policing the drunkenness amongst the naval ratings.

Above. The helmet plate badge used by the Devonport Borough force throughout its existence depicts the hull of a ship being built, showing the association with the established shipbuilding industry of Devonport.
(Jeff Cowdell)

Right. Two Devonport officers, W. Heath and A. Heath (father and son), wearing the pill box hat which was favoured by this force until helmets were introduced in 1901.

Above left. The tombstone of Constable John Yeo, an officer of the borough. The truncheon and rattle symbols were often to be found on police graves at this time. Sadly it is now in a neglected state, and in a cemetery in Plymouth city which risks having its gates closed due to lack of funding for maintenance.

Above right. A constable of Devonport, circa 1901, with the first pattern of helmet which replaced the former pill box hat. Many other forces at this time had already adopted the new style helmet for their officers, but the Devonport Borough Police had retained the pill box hat for a longer period. The style of helmet shown, however, is smaller than many of the period and, with just a cloth covered dome top, not particularly ornate.

Left. Constable Charles Nivey, photographed in about 1914, just prior to the amalgamation of the force into Plymouth Borough. He is seen here with a much more elaborate helmet which many forces were then adopting towards the years of the Great War.

Devonport Tug of War Team, 1908.

Rear Row: F. Pryor, A. Heath, F. Drake and L. Wully.
Seated in centre: W. Davey, J. Matters (Chief Constable) and F. Sandy (Team Captain),
Front Row: N. Holberton and W. Heath.

Below. A similar photograph of the borough force Tug of War team taken in 1911.

Above. A photograph of the Devonport Borough force taken in about 1908, complete with senior officers and detective.

Below. Devonport County Borough Police 1912. The last group photograph taken of this force prior to its amalgamation into the Plymouth Borough Police, in 1914.

Devonport County Borough Police, 1912.

Plymouth Borough Police
(1836 - 1928)

Although Plymouth in 1836 was considerably smaller than the large city of today, it was one of the first places to have its own force due to carrying the status of a county borough. Over the years that followed, the Plymouth Borough Police steadily increased in size and area and particularly so with the advent of the Great War in 1914, when, as already mentioned in the previous chapter, it took over the areas of Devonport and Stonehouse. However, once the status of 'City' had been conferred onto Plymouth in 1928, the name of its police force also changed - to 'Plymouth City Police'.

Right. The tombstone of Constable William Bennett. He was struck down whilst effecting the arrest of an offender after having served for less than two years in the force.

Such a tragedy is a poignant reminder that the dangers faced by police officers in today's police service are nothing new. How often it seems that many look back with nostalgia at "the good old days" of policing, but the reality was just as harsh as it is today.

A footnote to this story is that Constable Bennett's assailant was eventually found 'not guilty' of his murder. This was because the court heard that Bennett had followed his murderer to his home address in the city, and therefore, when the attack took place, Constable Bennett was said to have been a trespasser.

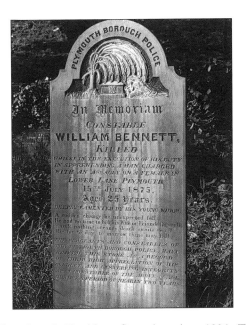

Left. Joseph Davidson Sowerby, circa 1894. The Chief Constable of Plymouth Borough Police from 1892 until his retirement in 1917 and, therefore, its senior officer during the amalgamation years of 1914, when the Devonport Borough Police and Stonehouse District of the Devon Constabulary merged into his force.

Mr Sowerby had been a senior officer in the service at Leeds until taking up his post as Chief Constable, and, like many other Chief Constables of that era, he was also the Chief Fire Officer for the Plymouth Fire Brigade. The ornate frock coat which he is wearing was favoured by most Chief Constables in the latter years of the Victorian age, and the badge on his pill box hat is the crest of the borough of Plymouth.

(Steve Gomersall)

Right. Constable 23 A. D. Damerell, photographed in about 1902, with the ornate ball-topped helmet used by the Plymouth Borough Police at that time - a very different figure to his colleagues in the neighbouring Devonport Borough Police who had only just, by this time, changed over to using the distinctive helmets from their former pill box hats. Seen next to his numbers on his collar is the crest of Plymouth County Borough, which was retained when the Plymouth Borough Police eventually changed its name to Plymouth City Police in 1928. However, whilst the collar-dog crest stayed the same, the actual helmet was changed for a slightly different pattern. The helmet plate badge also changed.

(Many helmet plates at that time were being changed to the new style of 'star' plate badges, similar to those on police helmets of today. But when the Borough Police changed its name, the new city force also opted to keep a crest - although with a slightly different design - as its helmet plate badge. In fact, it was not until the final amalgamation of the Plymouth force with the neighbouring counties in 1967 that a star plate badge was seen on the helmets of its officers. Instead, right up until the last moment, Plymouth retained great pride in its individual identity.)

Left. A second-class constable of the borough force, photographed in about 1908. Note the change in helmet style and the alteration to a crown beside the collar number instead of the Plymouth Borough crest. As has already been seen elsewhere in this volume, inverted chevrons on the cuffs of constables' tunics were often used to indicate class, merit and position within that rank.

The helmet plate badge remained the same, but the helmet changed to a much lower pattern than the one a few years previously. It was, of course, at this time that the relationship between Great Britain and our Germanic cousins was rather strained. Many police forces felt that the ornate helmets, which had originally been modelled on military helmets of the later Victorian times, were a little too 'Prussian', and not to the liking of the general public. This is a clear indication that then, as indeed now, the opinion of the public played a significant role in the manner in which they were policed, and how the police officers in their community were dressed - an assurance indeed that the status of the police officer has always been a citizen locally appointed, working within the local community, and supported by it.

Above. The Plymouth Borough Police had a strong rowing club, as seen here in about 1912. Many forces enjoyed well-represented sports clubs and associations, and, with Plymouth being a port, a rowing club was a natural recreation to attract the off-duty attentions of its officers.

Below. A fund-raising event of some description in about 1920, outside the Borough Police Headquarters.

Above. Photographed just prior to the Great War, this casually-posed borough group includes a rather puzzling image of a constable with flat cap and open neck coat with a collar and tie. His collar numbers on his lapel suggests that he is, in fact, a constable, but without a closed neck tunic this is rare indeed.

Below. A scuffle and arrest following the bread riots of 1924 during the depression in Plymouth.

Plymouth City Police
(1928 - 1967)

Having changed its name from the Plymouth Borough Police in 1928, this force continued to increase steadily in size and area over the years: as the city boundaries changed so the area of its police force followed suit. Moreover, parishes that were once policed by the Devon Constabulary slowly fell under the control of the city force as it stretched out into the surrounding countryside of Devonshire in order to accommodate an ever-enlarging population.

This situation, however, came to an abrupt halt in 1967, when the Plymouth City Police amalgamated with the neighbouring county forces and became part of the Devon & Cornwall Constabulary. Even so, the change was barely noticeable in many respects. Firstly, the majority of officers of the old city force declined to agree to serve outside the city, as was their right, and remained in Plymouth (which became a division of the new force): secondly, they also declined, for many years, to change uniforms (by choice rather than right!) - something that, no doubt, occurred elsewhere in the country upon numerous other amalgamations. Indeed, the officers of this former city force were still to be seen in their Plymouth uniforms and distinctive helmets as late as the 1980s.

Above. Constable 155 Hammacott. One of the first Plymouth City officers, pictured in 1929, shortly after the change from the borough force in the previous year. He is wearing the old pattern helmet, with cloth band, as well as a tunic belt. His whistle chain is also vertical with the whistle located in a small hidden pocket.

Above. The Chief Constable, circa 1930. Mr Archibald Wilson, Chief Constable of the Plymouth City Police, in his dress uniform. Later, in 1932, he became the Chief Constable of the City of Liverpool Police.

Above. This officer, photographed in about 1929, is Constable 54 who would have served with the former borough police prior to it becoming a city force. He is wearing the service medals of the Great War (the medal on his right breast would be a Royal Humane Society medal, or R.S.P.C.A. award) and also the new Plymouth City Police helmet plate badge which bore the ornate city crest.

(Richard Evans)

Above. The purpose for this Plymouth City Police parade through streets, not yet ravaged by the effect of the blitz, is unknown. However, the sergeants with the flat caps were motor patrol officers, who would have been stationed at the City Police Headquarters, at Greenbank.

Left. A photograph of the first motor patrol officers in the city, taken in about 1930 in the yard at their Greenbank Headquarters. Constable Edward Gibbs (see p.71) is the officer on the right.

As can be seen, little consideration was given to helmets or protective clothing for officers engaged in riding motorcycles in those days, although quite often they also wore greatcoats - with the rear flaps held up on hooks so as to prevent them from being caught up in the motorcycle's spokes! This aside, motorcycles were considered to be a far more efficient mode of quick transport for city forces than the less-manoeuvrable motor car.

(Jill Haynes)

Above. Pre-war city traffic congestion seen in about 1938. A lone officer is attempting to sort out a busy street corner before the age of traffic lights and roundabouts.

Above. Another busy street scene in a pre-war Plymouth. Along with many other cities, congestion involving traffic and pedestrians presented a major part of policing a beat, with the result that 'point duty' took up much of the officer's time whilst on patrol.

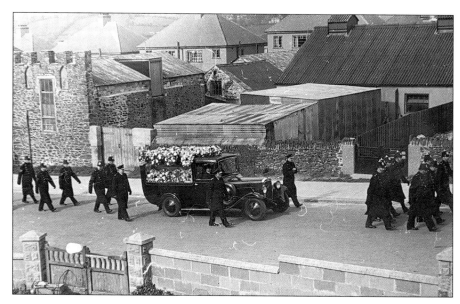

Above. An officer's funeral cortege, consisting of his colleagues from the force, winds its way through the city streets in the late 1930s.

The Blitz on Plymouth. It is a great tribute to the men and women of the Plymouth City Police, many of whom were destined to lose their lives, that they never failed to perform their duty in wartime conditions, especially when bearing in mind that they had, repeatedly, to face the effect of the nightly bombing. Indeed, what these officers witnessed - the huge amount of devastation and human carnage - is beyond the understanding of many of their modern-day counterparts.

In the photograph above an officer stands on a street corner talking to the occupants of a bombed residential area of the city, a scene typical of the constant horror that he and his colleagues had to endure.

Right. Sergeant Edward Harold Gibbs, photographed in the summer of 1940 upon his promotion to sergeant, when he was stationed at Devonport, near the dockyard. On 29th April 1941 a heavy air raid by German bombers took place on the docks, a common target. Sergeant Gibbs was in uniform and in the company of his brother, Sidney Gibbs, at that time the Head A.R.P. Warden, and Sidney's 14 year-old son, David, who was an A.R.P. messenger boy. Whilst at the junction of Corondale Road and Beacon Park Road in the city they were caught in the bombing and killed, a matter of yards from their homes.

(Sergeant Gibbs was the son-in-law of Constable Sidney Smallacombe, an officer of the former Devonport Borough Police, and his name appears on the Plymouth City Police war memorial along with other officers of the city whose lives were laid down in the name of the service. To many of a modern age these names often appear insignificant among the thousands of others on numerous memorials throughout the nation; but each name records a personal tragedy to a family, none more so than to those of Sergeant Gibbs and his brother.)

(Jill Haynes)

Author's note. This is the last photograph of Sergeant Gibbs that his daughter, now Mrs Jill Haynes, possesses of her father, saved from the wreckage of the blitz. I am grateful indeed for its loan.

Left. Officers of the Plymouth City 'Women's Auxiliary Police Service' in the central registry office at their Greenbank Headquarters of the city force. These ladies were affectionately referred to as 'WAPSies' by their male colleagues. Their duties included vital administrative and support functions during the troubled years of conflict and bombardment of the city. They 'manned' telephones and the force control room, and were, more than once, subjected to enemy bombs being dropped on the Mutley area of the city. At one point they were evacuated to temporary premises near Widey, on the outskirts of the city, which was thought to be a safer location for the wartime control room.

Wings for Victory Parade, 1943. Seen here marching down North Hill in the city, passing the museum and library, are officers of the city force taking part in the 'Wings for Victory' parade. **Above** are regular officers as well as members of the Special Constabulary and War Reserve Police. The female contingent, **below,** are members of the Plymouth City Police 'Women's Auxiliary Police Service'. (Note the tram-lines in the road, leading down to the city centre from Mutley Plain and the north of the city.)

Above. Constable 223 Charles Richards from Truro, on the left facing the camera. He was one of several Cornwall Constabulary officers billeted in the evacuated Royal Eye Infirmary building at Mutley after having been drafted in to help out their Plymouth City colleagues during the height of the blitz in about 1943. Pictured with him is a grim-faced Constable Ira Barrett, also from Truro, and, on the right, a Plymouth City war reserve constable. (The only illumination used to take this photograph was that from the burning buildings facing the officers.)

(Ret'd Sgt. Charles Richards)

Right. The memorial to the officers of the Plymouth City Police who lost their lives either in the city on duty or during military service overseas.

Many officers from the city force volunteered to join the armed services during the war, hence the need to bring in the war reserve and first reserve officers back from retirement, and into their old familiar uniforms.

1939 · 1945

TO the LASTING MEMORY of
BRAVE MEN MEMBERS of THE
PLYMOUTH
CITY POLICE FORCE
WHO FELL EITHER in THIS
CITY or OVERSEAS in THE
WORLD WAR

REGULAR POLICE
W J BROOKS
R A CHILCOTT DFC
J T G GERRETTY
E H GIBBS
R W SANDOVER
W T SANDOVER
K J WALTERS
N E WEST

FIRST POLICE
RESERVE
W J CHEEK
A E CROSBY

SPECIAL
CONSTABULARY
S J H BAKER
W J A BEER
S J B HANNAM
A E HARRIS
W J K HUTCHINGS

POLICE WAR
RESERVE
W D STRIBLEY
L C VICKERY
W WHITE

And two things have altered not
Since first the world began
The beauty of the wild green earth
And the bravery of man

Above. A traffic motorcyclist of the city force taking part in the 'Victory in Europe' parade. (Note the headlamp guard to prevent too much light from being shown which might, unwittingly, provide a signal to enemy aircraft.)

An inspection by Her Majesty's Inspector of Constabulary in the yard of Greenbank Police Headquarters shortly after the end of the war.

Return of HMS Amethyst, 1949. Following the 'Yangzce' incident, tens of thousands of Plymouth residents turned out to welcome home HMS Amethyst. This picture, taken in Old Town Street, Plymouth, where wartime bomb damage is still very much in evidence, shows the emotion and excitement of the welcome afforded the crew. The reader surely can't help but wonder if a line of policemen with a rope could keep back such a crowd nowadays!

Force Parade, 1950. Being inspected by Her Majesty's Inspector of Constabulary are the city force in the Headquarters yard - formed up with 'B' division (Greenbank) in the front, 'A' division (Crownhill) in the middle and 'C' division (Devonport) at the rear.

With thanks to Bill Swales who supplied this picture, some of the names of the officers of the 'B' division are:-

Front rank:- Inspectors Poole and Dick Screech.
Second rank:- Sergeant Jack Parish and Constables Vic Collins, Ernie Wickstead, Fred Povey, Frank Naughton GC, Fern Cousins, Don Potter, Arthur Crisp, Bill Swales, Des Monk, Don Bulley, George Tembeath, Dave Morgan, Bob Phippen, Len Kelly and Les Richards.
Third rank:- unknown, unknown, Jim Douglas, Doug Gilbert, Den Williams, Bill Cawse, Stan Marks, Jack Cockburn, unknown, Jim Cowling, Ben Freud, unknown, unknown, Jack Trudgeon, Arthur Tait, Jim McKelvey, unknown and Ray Tapper.
Fourth rank:- Sergeants Les Wallace and Len Malin.

(Constable Frank Naughton GC, in the second rank, is the only holder of the George Cross ever to serve in any force in the area now covered by the Devon & Cornwall Constabulary. His former award of the Empire Gallantry Medal - awarded for gallantry during the 1939-1945 war whilst serving with the Tank Regiment - was exchanged for the George Cross when this later medal was established at the end of the war).

(Bill Swales)

Above. Class 27 of February 1948 at the Police Training Centre at Falfield near Bristol, which officers from all of the South West forces attended for their initial training. Constable David Scoble of the Plymouth City Police is seen in the back row, in the centre, with the distinctive Plymouth City Police helmet; the constables in the flat caps are from Dorset Police, who wore no helmets at that time; the two officers in front of Constable Scoble are from the Cornwall Constabulary; the Commandant, in the centre of the front row, is Superintendent Thurley-Beale of the Plymouth City Police; and the other officers are from the Gloucestershire Constabulary, and the Somerset & Bath Police.

(Ret'd Superintendent David Scoble)

Below right. The Lord Mayor of the city inspecting officers wearing the new style open neck tunics in the early 1950s.

Below left. The final queen's crown helmet plate badge and 'collar dogs' worn by the Plymouth City Police. Much sought after by collectors of police insignia, the Plymouth City Police badge with a queen's crown is a rare find indeed.

(Dave Wilkinson)

Above. Constable Peter Pope, pictured in the early 1960s in Keyham Road, in the Devonport area of the city, on a Velocette 197cc water-cooled motorcycle. This machine was used by officers for patrolling the outlying areas of the city, and was chosen because of its very quiet engine, particularly for night patrol. Finished in police blue, it had a loudspeaker on the handle bar and a radio behind the single seat.

(Peter Pope)

Above. Constable Alan Dewdney, pictured in the yard of the old Crownhill Police Station, long since demolished. This photograph was taken in about 1967, just prior to the end of the Plymouth City Police, and Constable Dewdney used the motorcycle to cover out into the rural part of the city force limits. (Areas such as Estover and Southway were, at that time, in the countryside, and the Plymouth City force's northern boundary with its Devon Constabulary neighbours was at Roborough village.)

(Alan Dewdney)

Left. Sergeant David Scoble, pictured in the early 1960s outside the city centre police station, which is situated near the present civic centre. (The old city centre station buildings now house the Crown Court offices.) He is seen here wearing both a St. John's First Aid badge as well as a Royal Lifesaving Society bronze medallion.

Officers of the Plymouth force were required to have the extra bronze medallion because of the fact that, being a port town and on the coast, so much of their force area was surrounded by water. Indeed, there are numerous instances recorded of officers who had to jump into water to save life, and it was felt, at that time, that a non-swimming officer would be of no operational use.

(Ret'd Superintendent David Scoble)

The Final Parade.

Above. Plymouth City Police Cadets prepare to march off as part of the large final parade of the Plymouth City Police in 1967, just prior to its amalgamation into the Devon & Cornwall Constabulary.

Right. The officers of the former 'Policewomen's Department' of the force, seen here as they enter Royal Parade. Many Plymouthians speak of this final parade as a magnificent occasion even though, because of the crowd, there was hardly enough room to stand anywhere along the whole length of Royal Parade, in the centre of the city, to view the proceedings.

Above. Led by the Deputy Chief Constable, the head of the final march past of the Plymouth City Police passes along Royal Parade in the city centre.

Below. The motor patrol, and unit beat contingent, of the parade passing by the saluting dais outside the guildhall.

DEVON COUNTY
Barnstaple Borough Police
(1836 - 1921)

Barnstaple, the 'capital' of North Devon, well deserved its own force, and was soon to follow suit with other large towns when its borough police was formed in 1836, taking over from the solitary, rather hard-pressed parish officer. Initially, it had a superintendent as its senior officer, but this rank was changed to Chief Constable in 1872.

In 1893 Richard Eddy was appointed Chief Constable, and when he retired in 1905 his son, Richard Sidney Eddy, succeeded him. Mr Eddy then remained in charge until 1st October 1921, when the Barnstaple Borough Police amalgamated with the Devon Constabulary, and subsequently became a superintendent at Barnstaple in charge of the 'A' division, which covered North Devon. Later, he moved to the Torquay area.

Above. A Barnstaple Borough constable stands in the High Street of the town in about 1910. On his left cuff he is wearing a 'duty band' which is a rarity indeed, as very few forces in the South West used these bands; they were an indication as to whether the officer was on or off duty. (Even when off duty, officers were still required to wear uniforms much of the time.)

(Trevor Finbow)

Right. The helmet plate badge of the Barnstaple Borough force, depicting a castle surrounded by laurel leaves and topped with the royal crown.

(Dave Wilkinson)

Barnstaple Borough Police, 1908.

A photograph taken in the yard at the rear of the station in Barnstaple showing the officers of the borough force with their Chief Constable, Richard Sidney Eddy.

The last of the Barnstaple Borough Police - 1921.

The Chief Constable, R. S. Eddy, is pictured here in the last photograph of the force, taken in the pannier market in the town. He is accompanied by Sergeants Charles Smith and Bartholomew Braund, along with Constables William Manley, James Squires, John Fry, John Brownscombe, John Corney, William Taylor, John Newcombe, Alfred Hill, Walter Baker, Sidney Gould and Samuel Gammon. All of these officers transferred to the Devon Constabulary on 1st October 1921 and were permitted to remain in the Barnstaple area, which was often the case with the small borough forces upon amalgamation.

Left. This picture shows the large procession and attendance at the funeral of Superintendent Richard Sidney Eddy, of Torquay, in 1929. It was he who was the last Chief Constable of the Barnstaple Borough force, up until its amalgamation into the Devon Constabulary.

Bideford Borough Police
(1836 - 1889)

A letter of 29th July 1836 from the Bideford Town Clerk to the Commissioners of the Metropolitan Police enquired whether a trained officer could be provided by the Metropolitan Police for the purposes of superintending the police at Bideford. The commissioners agreed, and on 22nd August that year Elias Palmer arrived from London to take over the policing of the borough, on condition that he "be issued with lantern, staff and rattle." On 19th May 1889 the Chief Constable of the Devon Constabulary reported that David Morgan, Head Constable of Bideford Borough Police, had been offered an appointment as a sergeant in the county force, and had accepted the offer on the understanding that he suffered no pecuniary loss. Until this time Bideford had maintained one head constable and two constables in its borough force, and so ended the life of yet another of the smaller borough forces in the county.

Left. The helmet plate badge of the Bideford Borough Police. The crest in the centre is of a high masted ship passing through the arch of the long bridge which spans the River Torridge, and the crown is a queen's crown from the reign of Victoria.

This is a photograph of possibly the only surviving Bideford Borough badge in existence, held at the Metropolitan Police Museum in London, even though similar examples were used in numerous situations throughout this port town. Indeed, up until 1975, it was used as the blazer badge for the local Bideford Grammar School (which the author would unashamedly declare great affection for!).

(The Metropolitan Police Museum)

Tavistock Borough Police
(1837 - 1856)

The local Duke of Bedford was a most influential landowner in West Devon, and it was he who instructed his agent to contact the newly-formed Metropolitan Police with a view to having an officer sent to the town to advise in the formation of a new police force. Shortly after the arrival of the London officer, the Tavistock Borough force was created.

The duke had the officers housed in the old guildhall, but this was soon to prove too small for their purposes. So, at the duke's instigation, a new police station (and guildhall) was built, amidst the ruins of the old Tavistock Abbey, and this was opened in 1847. Since then Tavistock Police Station has remained in the same building, and, as such, is the oldest police station in the Westcountry, as well as being the second oldest in England. This is in spite of the fact that once the new Devon Constabulary had been formed in 1856 the town's policing requirements were provided by the county force, and the Tavistock Borough force was disbanded. A statue of the generous duke, incidentally, stands in the station car park as a fitting memorial.

Tavistock Police Station, circa 1899.

Built in 1847 for the borough force, the Tavistock Guildhall also housed the Quarter Sessions Court as well as the local 'Fire Engine Station'. The area outside of the building once held the local sheep market, but nowadays it acts as a car park. With the exception of the addition of vehicles, the view above, which includes the Duke of Bedford's statue, has remained unchanged over the last century.

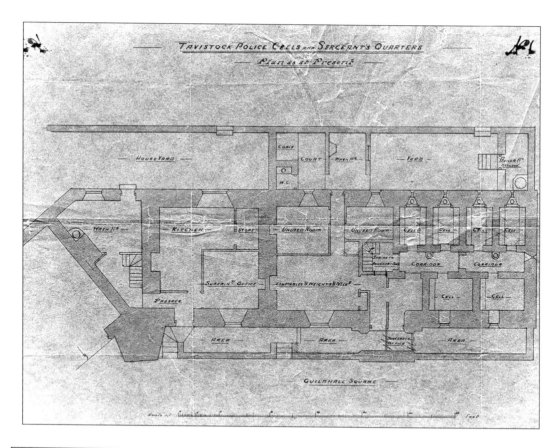

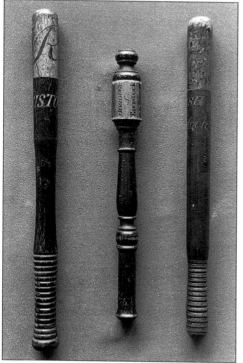

Above. Plans of the police station of 1890. The building had remained unchanged from when it was inherited from the borough force, but in July 1890 the nearby River Tavy burst its banks and the basement rooms were flooded to a depth of over six feet, necessitating the rescue of prisoners trapped in their cells. These same cells then became unfit to hold prisoners, who, for two years, had to be transported to the cells at Lifton Police Station, about nine miles to the north.

(Tavistock Museum)

Left. A small selection of 'borough truncheons' of Tavistock held at the town's museum. As mentioned previously, these types of truncheons were the badges of office of the parish and, later, borough officers before they were issued with uniforms. Not only are there a number of these on display in Tavistock's museum, but a greater collection is held in the mayor's parlour of this historic town. It can be seen that the earliest truncheon (on the right) displays the words 'Parish of Tavistock', later to be changed and upgraded to 'Borough of Tavistock'.

(Tavistock Museum)

Tiverton Borough Police
(1845 - 1943)

Tiverton Borough Police was formed at around the same time as many other borough forces, in 1845, and went on to have the distinction of being the last remaining old borough force in the county to be amalgamated with the Devon Constabulary. That was on 1st January 1943, after 98 years of service, at which time it was the smallest borough force in the country, with just eleven officers, despite having the largest acreage of any borough to police.

Upon amalgamation the Chief Constable, Mr B. M. Beynon, became superintendent of the new 'C' division of the Devon Constabulary, which had its Headquarters at Tiverton. Consequently, like the former Chief Constable of the Barnstaple Borough Police in 1921, Mr Beynon didn't have to leave his old force area.

BOROUGH OF TIVERTON.

POLICEMAN
WANTED.

An Active Young Man between 25 and 35 Years of Age, Height not under 5 feet 9 inches, is required in the Police Force of this Borough, *Salary 19s. per Week.*

TESTIMONIALS TO CHARACTER must be sent to the Town Clerk's Office, on or before Tuesday the 10th of August next, and Applicants are desired to attend at the Guildhall, on Wednesday the 11th of August at Eleven o'clock in the Forenoon.

By order of the Watch Committee,

C. M. HOLE,
TOWN CLERK.

Town Clerk's Office, Tiverton 26th July, 1869.

MEAD, PRINTER, GOLD STREET, TIVERTON.

Borough of Tiverton recruiting poster. A typical vacancy advertisement of the day, by the order of the 'Watch Committee', the forerunner to the modern-day police authority.

Above. Tiverton Borough Police, circa 1898. This photograph, which includes Chief Constable J. Blechynden Crabb, shows that the force consisted of one sergeant, an acting sergeant (with two chevrons) and eight constables. Rare for a Westcountry force, the Tiverton constables are shown wearing 'duty bands' on the left cuffs of their tunics. Their ornate collar designs, on the other hand, are typical of the 19th century.

(Jeff Cowdell)

Below. The first helmet plate badge of the Tiverton force. In common with many other constabularies at the time, early badges bore the Victorian crown and name of the force, but had a plain centre.

(Metropolitan Police Museum)

Left. Constable Perry, pictured in about 1881, with his family.
(Jeff Cowdell)

Above. The force helmet plate badge of about 1890, which had a Victorian crown and a more ornate design than the previous badge. This design, however, did not last many years, as it was changed to reflect a more appropriate image of the borough of Tiverton.

Above. A photograph of the Chief Constable, Henry Charles Rawle, taken in about 1910. At this time Chief Constables in the smaller borough forces also doubled as the fire chief for the area, as many of them had become combined 'police fire services'.

Below right. Taken in the late 1920s, this picture shows the borough Chief Constable, Mervyn Beynon, at a children's carnival in the town park. He is with Sergeant Frederick Williams (on the right) and Constable Arthur Chidgey.

(Fred Williams)

Below left. A king's crown helmet plate badge and 'collar dogs', bearing the borough crest.

(Dave Wilkinson)

Right. Inspector Perry, with Constable Takle, photographed on horseback in the rear yard of Tiverton Police Station in about 1915. The horses which the force normally used were loaned from the Borough Corporation: their usual daily job, though, was that of hauling the corporation dustcart, the shafts of which can be seen to the left of the picture.

Occasionally another source of horses used by the force, which owned its own tack, was from the stables of the nearby Palmerston Hotel.

Left. Sergeant Frederick Williams seen here on horseback at the Devon County Show in 1925, which, that year, was held at Tiverton. Sergeant Williams performed almost all his duties in the Tiverton force, after active service in the Great War, only leaving upon transferring to the Devon Constabulary, as a sergeant, following the 1943 amalgamation.

On this occasion Sergeant Williams is using a horse on loan from Sir John Amory, and it is rather odd to note that he is wearing a peaked cap. Indeed, this fact has remained a mystery, because at that time constables and sergeants usually wore helmets, whereas flat caps were invariably reserved for such ranks when engaged on motor patrol duties.

(Fred Williams)

Right. A procession in the borough, pictured in about 1920. The mace bearers for the Tiverton Borough were usually the local town sergeants, although in this view the officer on the right is recently promoted Acting Sergeant Takle, with two chevrons on his right sleeve.

The sergeants were paid for these extra duties on ceremonial occasions, which they undertook very seriously and with a great degree of pride and dignity.

Left. This photograph, taken in the late 1920s, shows a group of officers outside Tiverton Town Hall, which includes (on the left) Acting Sergeant Takle. It was a peculiarity of the Tiverton Borough force that when a constable was approaching retirement age he was promoted to acting sergeant in order that he could enhance his pension somewhat: there are a number of instances of such promotions just prior to retirement for this purpose. The officer on the right, meanwhile, is Constable Elston, renowned for numerous unkind nicknames given to him by the residents of Tiverton, including the somewhat irreverent one of 'Creeping Jesus'. One of his individual peculiarities was to wear his whistle chain in his left pocket contrary to orders!

Right. Another procession, this time in the 1930s and being led by the Chief Constable, with the sergeant mace-bearers. The sergeant on the left is Frederick Williams, whose son, Fred Williams, joined the Exeter City Police as a messenger boy clerk and later became a constable in the Southampton Borough Police.

(Fred Williams)

Left. The proclamation of the succession to the throne of King Edward VIII in 1936, outside Tiverton Town Hall - an event preceded by a heavy snow shower, as can be seen from the soldiers' caps in the foreground. Again, as this was a ceremonial occasion, the borough sergeants acted as mace-bearers, and the Chief Constable is also in attendance. Sergeant Frederick Williams is pictured on the right.

Such significant proclamations were always afforded this formality and were regarded as quite an occasion in the borough.

(Fred Williams)

The Tiverton Borough Police, prior to its amalgamation in the January of 1943.

Rear row (standing, left to right): Special Constable Bennett (a retired Inspector from the Metropolitan Police), Constables Frank Harding, Stan Edwards, Bill Stuckey, Sid Badcock (later an Inspector in the Devon county force), Arthur Chidgey and Jack Squires, and Special Constable Morrell. Front row (seated, left to right): Acting Sergeant Bill Land, Sergeant Frank Galpin, Chief Constable Mervyn Beynon, Sergeant Frederick Williams and Constable Cyril Richards. (Cyril Richards later became the borough's first and only Detective Constable. Later still, he served as a Detective Inspector in the Devon county force.)

It is interesting to note that, by the 1940s, whistle chains were worn into the left breast pocket.

Devon Constabulary
(1856 - 1966)

For many years up until the mid-19th century the policing of Devonshire fell to the unpaid, locally-appointed parish constables in its numerous villages and towns, or to paid and uniformed borough and city policemen in the larger areas of population. However, the 'County Police Acts' of 1839 and 1840 laid down requirements, nationally, for counties to adopt properly run county constabularies, and eventually, in 1856, it was this that led to the creation of the Devon Constabulary.

Over the years that followed many of the smaller and 'inefficient' borough police forces were gradually taken over by the county force until, by 1947, the Devon Constabulary had amalgamated with all the other forces in the county, with the exception of those in the cities of Plymouth and Exeter. As time continued to march on, though, so developed a trend, nationally, of creating even larger constabularies, and in the mid-1960s it was decided that the counties of Devon and Cornwall, along with the two city police forces of Plymouth and Exeter, would amalgamate; the first amalgamation to take place, on 1st October 1966, being the Devon Constabulary with the Exeter City Police to form the Devon & Exeter Police. This, of course, marked the end of an era in the policing of Devon, although, as in many other instances, the badges and uniforms of the old Devon county force were not to vanish from daily use until several years later.

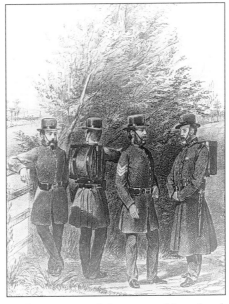

Above. Senior officers of the Devon Constabulary, from a drawing of 1871. The officers wore the distinctive 'pill box hat' for many years, along with frock coats.

Most superintendents were allocated a constable to act as groom for their horses. This constable, however, would still be responsible for routine patrol duties in the same manner as his colleagues.

Above. A sergeant and three constables, also dated about 1871. These officers wore the low brimmed hat with chin strap, as well as long frock coats. In addition, the constables often wore haversacks to carry essentials whilst they walked their long beats, and also had a truncheon hung from their belt, as can be seen from the officer to the right.

Above. Superintendent William Mitchell, photographed in about 1880 with his family. Mitchell was, at that time, the superintendent of the Tavistock 'K' division. His son, Arthur, seen seated on the left, also became a policeman when he joined the Metropolitan Police, and it was he, as a detective sergeant in 1910, who crossed the Atlantic to arrest the murderer, Doctor Crippen.

(Mrs Launa Mitchell)

Below. The Devon Constabulary was one of the few forces to have an officer of the rank of sergeant major (responsible for training recruits), and he is depicted here at Headquarters in about 1888. The officer in the rear row, third from the left, is Constable (later Superintendent) Edward Shutler.

(John Shutler)

Constable John Cousins and family, circa 1897. This remarkable family photograph was taken in the rear yard of the Halwill police cottage, near Holsworthy. Constable Cousins is pictured with his wife, Ann, and their eight daughters. The girls names and years of birth are, from left to right: Annie 1885, Violet 1886, Florrie 1888, Minnie 1889, Katie 1891, Hetty 1892, Louisa 1894 and Margaret 1896. The following year the family moved to Tawstock, near Barnstaple, where two boys were born - Jack in 1898 and Charles in 1899.

Above. Pictured in about 1879 in their new 'Pickelhaub' helmets are Sergeant James Richards and Constables Robert Brock, James Mitchell, George Frost (the three standing, left to right), William Piller and Charles Gidley.

Above. First-class Constable T. Crooke, with 'merit stripe' above his class chevrons. He was stationed at a village post in the Holsworthy division, circa 1891.

Below. The superintendent and officers of the Holsworthy 'L' division in about 1895.

Torquay 'F' Division, circa 1899. For over a century the Torquay division was always the 'F' division, right up until the modern times of the Devon & Cornwall Constabulary. This photograph is typical of the size of such a division, with senior officers still in their pill box caps. The gentleman in the bowler hat is a detective. In the rear row, second from the left, is a young Constable Potter, the great grandson of the last parish constable at Abbotskerswell, pictured on page 13. It was one of his daughters who was the prison warderess who sat with Ruth Ellis, the last woman to be hanged in Britain, on the eve of her execution.

(Mrs Frances Peek)

DEVON CONSTABULARY, A Division, May, 1903.

P.C. MARTIN. (Berrynarbor.)	P.C. CHADDER. (Ilfracombe.)	P.C. HOLMAN. (Braunton.)	P.C. NANCEKIVELL. (Instow.)	P.C. MULES. (Georgeham.)	P.C. COUSINS. (Tawstock.)	P.C. BIRRINGS. (Lynton.)	P.C. BRAUND. (Ilfracombe.)
P.C. AVANT. (Barnstaple.)	P.C. BROCK. (Parracombe.)	P.C. SELDON. (Bishopstawton.)	P.C. MOGGRIDGE. (Sherwill.)	P.C. LABDON. (Ilfracombe.)	P.C. FISHLEIGH. (Wesadown.)	P.C. WATTS. (Swymbridge.)	P.C. MARCHANT. (Ilfracombe.)	P.C. LEACH. (Combemartin.)
P.C. HED'LAND. (Marwood.)	P.S. ROUSE. (Braunton.)	P.S. JEFFERY. (Ilfracombe.)	Supt. HOBBS. (Barnstaple.)	P.S. KING. (Landkey.)	P.S. ADAMS. (Parracombe.)	P.C. SCREECH. (Bratton Fleming.)	P.C. CRAGO. (Fremington.)

The Barnstaple Division, 1903. The Devon Constabulary had a superintendent at Barnstaple in charge of the North Devon 'A' division, although at this time there was still a Barnstaple Borough Police: the borough force took care of the town of Barnstaple and the constable of the Devon Constabulary stationed at Barnstaple, with his superintendent, did local duties and acted as groom.

Exeter Division, late 1903. Although there was an Exeter City Police force, the Devon Constabulary's 'X' division was based in Exeter (which had the status of a county borough) and policed the city's outskirts.

By late 1903 the old 'Pickelhaub' helmets had fallen from favour, being too similar to the Prussian military helmet, and, instead, the Boar War bush hat (or slouch hat, as it was known) was brought into use: the Devon Constabulary was one of only four forces in the country to use this style of hat. Note also the officer's number and divisional letter still being worn on collars.

Left. A photograph of Constable 388 James Jury, with his daughter, taken in about 1904 outside his Elburton police house, near Plymstock. His 'collar number' and divisional letter have been moved to his epaulette and replaced, at the neck, by a crown.

The distinctive 'Devon Constabulary' sign also appeared over the front door of cottages and stations, whether owned or rented by the county constabulary. This sign included the divisional letter of the station and also the 'collar number' of the constable or sergeant stationed there. (For stations which had the rank of inspector or above, the rank of the most senior officer at that station was displayed instead of a number - at Divisional Headquarters this showed the rank of 'Superintendent'.)

Below left. Taken in about 1904, this photograph of Constable Voaden shows clearly the crown being worn at the neck in place of the 'collar number', which is where it remained right up until the introduction of open neck tunics many years later.

Below right. The King Edward VII helmet plate badge. This would have appeared on the slouch hats, on the turned-up side, and also on the helmets, which were reintroduced a few years into the reign of Edward VII.

(Jeff Cowdell)

Above. Constable Horn, photographed outside his picturesque police cottage in Rock Walk, at Torquay, in about 1905. This small dwelling on the seafront, built into the cliff bottom, must surely have been situated in one of the most attractive locations for a station.

Below. The funeral procession of the great hero of the Zulu wars, General Sir Redvers Buller VC, being led by a small detachment of the Devon Constabulary, with the aptly-named Sergeant-Major Thomas Major at its head. General Buller was buried at Crediton amid great ceremony, and a fine statue of him on horseback is situated in Exeter.

(Mrs Jean Major)

A street scene in Bideford, circa 1907. A public gathering for some notable event, this photograph captures a great social scene and the fashion of the Edwardian era. The police officers still have their whistle chains entering the right pocket, but for a brief time the chains entered on the outside of the button. The St. John's First Aid badge is also clearly to be seen on the right sleeves of these constables, and the white gloves worn by the officers suggest that the event was of some importance.

Above. Budleigh Salterton Police Station, circa 1908. Seen in the final year of the slouch hat, this station, situated near Exmouth, was a 'sergeant station'. Therefore, the number of the sergeant appears above the front door on the sign.

When an officer joined the force, or upon promotion, he was issued with a number on a piece of wood which he slotted into the sign over his front door upon taking up residence with his family at a new station. In this photograph, which shows the sergeant with chevrons only on his right sleeve (they did not have chevrons on both sleeves until the 1930s), the constable was either an unmarried officer in lodgings or a married man with a police house elsewhere in the town.

Right. Constable 28 Fred Phillips and his wife, Gertrude, pictured in about 1909 outside their Otterton village police thatched cottage (in the 'X' division) in East Devon. Constable Phillips is seen with his brand new, much-prized silver pedal cycle. He had come into some money from an inheritance and decided to make his life a little easier by investing in a new cycle. Unfortunately, though, his superintendent had not taken kindly to a constable coming into such wealth and decided to forbid him from riding it. The superintendent had decided that such a distinctive cycle would indicate the presence of the constable and be detrimental to efficient police duties!

(Mrs Molly Walker)

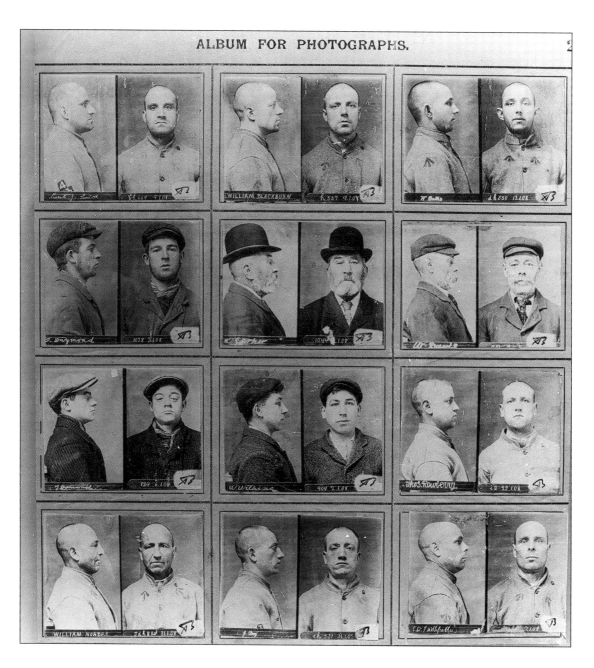

Prisoner's photographic album, circa 1908. This page, from a Devon Constabulary prisoner's photographic album, clearly shows how the development of photography played such an important role in policing. The faces might seem to have been lifted right from the pages of Charles Dickens' *Great Expectations*, but nevertheless provide an image of crime not often seen by the public.

The photographing of prisoners is still carried out in a very similar style to that of almost a century ago, although the gentlemen in hats would be invited to remove them nowadays!

Right. Constable James Stoneman. Seen here in about 1912 wearing the uniform of the Plymouth Fire Brigade, as the initials 'PFB' on his chest indicate, he was stationed at the police fire station in Laira, Plymouth, which now houses the local library.

Until comparatively recently the fire brigade in Plymouth city consisted of policemen who had dual duties. However, he was a Devon Constabulary constable, because that area of Plymouth was then policed by the county force as opposed to the city police.

(Mrs M. Steer)

Below left. A King George V helmet plate badge, dated about 1911, not long after the coronation. The Devon Constabulary never took to using the new style star helmet plate, but retained the laurel leaves surrounding the royal cipher.

Many helmet plate badges of this era were mainly black and only a few depicted the royal cipher in chrome.

(Jeff Cowdell)

Below right. The previous black plate was changed in favour of a different design towards the 1930s; this retained the very distinctive laurel leaves, but had more chrome.

(Jeff Cowdell)

Above. Officers on horseback, 1910. Taken on the occasion of the Mid-Devon elections, this photograph shows some of the officers who were used to patrol and visit the various polling stations around the rural areas of central Devon.

Below. Trevisco Clay Strike, 1913. Officers of the Devon Constabulary pictured at Trevisco quarry, near St. Austell. Like officers from other forces, they were providing assistance to their Cornish colleagues during the industrial unrest amongst the miners at that time.

Above. Men of the Devon Constabulary pictured in 1914 when they joined the Police Battery at Bristol. They formed part of the Heavy Regiment Royal Garrison Artillery and were used to pull the heavy guns at Ypres. Constable Fred Connett of Whitchurch, near Tavistock, is pictured in the back row - third from the left.

(Mr D. Connett)

Below. Pictured in about 1919, this lorry was used to relocate officers to new country beat stations around Devon, with their families and furniture - a frequent occurrence in those days.

Left. Constable 296 Rowland E. Hoare, pictured outside his police cottage in about 1914, in the 'L' (Holsworthy) division, accompanied by his wife, Laura, and son, also named Rowland. By this time the tradition of having inverted chevrons on the sleeves of constables' tunics had been stopped, as otherwise Constable Hoare's grade as a first-class constable would have been denoted by two inverted chevrons.

From Constable Hoare's service record, held at the police archives in Exeter, it can be seen that when he joined the Devon Constabulary on 29th November 1904 he was a third-class constable and, as such, would then have worn the 'bush hat' style of head dress. Later, on 29th November 1906, he was appointed a second-class constable, which would be similar to an officer of today completing his probationary period, before becoming a first-class constable on his fourth anniversary of joining the force. Finally, he retired with 26 years service in 1930, after having been awarded, in 1919, the class of 'merit', which was for meritorious service as opposed to length of service.

Right. Constable 178 Beer, pictured in about 1922 at Torquay, and seen here wearing puttees which were used for a short while after the Great War years in Devon. Behind him is one of the wooden 'Police Boxes' introduced in Torquay to assist the large numbers of officers on foot patrol in this heavily populated area, especially during the busy summer months. In fact, the Chief Constable had had eleven such boxes established in the locality at a cost of £157, and the lighting for them was provided by the Torquay Town Council.

The badge which Constable Beer has on his helmet is the black one shown previously on page 105, with the chrome royal cipher in the middle. It will be noted, however, that he is not wearing any chin strap. This is because from the 1920s, during the summer months, officers were permitted the small concession of not having to wear their chin straps down. (It was at Torquay that in the 1960s the first all-white police helmet was introduced as an experiment during the summer months. This was only a trial and the white helmet was not widely introduced or adopted for general wear - not many forces in the country experimented with such radical changes in their uniform styles!)

Above. Constable George Davis, pictured in 1926 on the front lawn of the Portsmouth Arms, near Umberleigh in North Devon, with the licensee's teenage daughter! Constable Davis was, at this time, stationed at the nearby Chulmleigh station and his cycle beat would have included the main Exeter to Barnstaple road, which is where the Portsmouth Arms is situated. It would have been usual for the local constable to make a routine visit to the licensed premises on his beat, but to provide self-defence lessons to the young daughter of a publican was a most unusual pastime. What his sergeant would have made of this rather odd behaviour is left for the reader to wonder at! The picture does, however, give a good indication of exactly what was worn under those high necked tunics - except that the retired country policemen of the day have even admitted to wearing pyjama jackets in the winter on their beats in an attempt to keep out the cold, or when called from their beds at night!

(Mrs Anne Blight)

Right. Sergeant Ernest Venton, pictured in about 1925 on his cycle at South Molton, a town which up until the late 1880s boasted a borough force.
In the 1920s the usual mode of transport for sergeants to visit their country beat constables would have been a cycle such as the one pictured.

(Mrs Joan Venton)

Above. This unfortunate constable who fainted on parade unwittingly provided the photographer with a rather unique and unexpected picture.

Below. The well-trained rural beat constable could turn his hand to the most unusual of duties as this officer in South Devon clearly displays in the late 1920s.

Commander Evangeline Booth, 1925. The handwriting on the reverse of this photograph states "Commander Evangeline Booth at Torquay Police Station, where she was arrested with other members of the Salvation Army 37 years ago for playing their instruments in the street on Sunday", but the *Devon Weekly Times* of 11th May 1888, had reported the initial incident involving the arrest and prosecution of Miss Booth for leading a procession in the harbour area of the town, with instruments, contrary to the 'Harbour Act'.

The photograph itself clearly shows the Devon Constabulary sign bearing the word 'Superintendent', this rank being that of the senior officer stationed at Torquay - Headquarters for the division.

Dartmoor Prison Mutiny, 1932 - officers of the Devon Constabulary drafted in to support their local colleagues during the infamous 1932 mutiny at Dartmoor Prison. They are pictured here having completed their duties and preparing to return to their respective stations.

Above. Officers, pictured in 1932 at Princetown, carrying exhibits to be shown at the temporary Assize Court in the local town hall, where the Dartmoor Prison mutineers were being tried. Among them is Constable Phillips who can be seen carrying the rope which the riotous prisoners had intended using, at some time, to hang the prison governor.

Such was the violent disposition of the prisoners that armed officers were posted around the building and a local blacksmith was employed to make a stout rail, to which the prisoners were shackled whilst in the court.

Right. Constable Harry Fice carefully inspects the documents of a motorist whilst his armed colleague looks on. They are shown in about 1932 at a prison escape check-point on the road leading towards Moretonhampstead from Princetown.

When a convict had escaped from Dartmoor Prison a massive scheme was put into operation to try to recapture him before he left the county boundary.

113

Above. The Devon Constabulary wartime operations room seen in about 1940. It was situated at the force Headquarters at Middlemoor, Exeter, behind sand-bagged windows in case of attack.

Below. Torquay railway station in 1939, where Sergeant Harry Gale is seen supervising the reception of young evacuees to the Westcountry. Apart from serving as a rather poignant reminder of the trauma that these children went through after being separated from their families in the cities, this photograph also shows that by 1939 sergeants were wearing chevrons on both arms.

(Mr K. E. Gale)

Right. Constable Arthur Lemon, carrying his gas mask bag, pictured in 1940 outside a well fortified Okehampton Police Station. This large station was the Divisional Headquarters of the 'B' division and, as such, was regarded as an important potential target for enemy attack.

By then the helmet plate badges were all chrome.

Below. This photograph, dated on the rear as 4th February 1948, shows Sergeant Climo from the Hoops station (near Clovelly) and the local constable after they had been involved in recovering a stranded bullock, trapped 550 feet down the high cliffs near Bucks Mills, in North Devon. Also included in the photograph is Inspector T. Crook of the R.S.P.C.A., on the left, who looks on as workmen tend to the exhausted animal and prepare a makeshift windbreak for it. The entire operation took five hours to complete and, judging by the state of the police officers, it would seem that they, too, were (justifiably) exhausted. The duties of the rural officer were indeed varied!

Above. A map dated 1948 showing the disposition of all the Devon Constabulary detached stations and sergeant stations, and also Divisional Headquarters.

Left. Constable 49 Charles Troake, photographed in 1948. When he joined the force, not long after the Second World War, he recalls that his older colleagues taught him always to carry a quantity of fox hair in his wallet! The reason for this was that chicken thieves were the bane of the village policeman's life, and were often responsible for an explosion of undetected crime. So, in order to 'assist' in keeping down the crime statistics for his beat, Constable Troake would sprinkle a few fox hairs around the scene of a poultry theft so as to ensure that a fox would be recorded as the offender, thus doing away with the need for the completion of a crime report!

During his police career Charles Troake also became one of the founders of the Devon & Cornwall Constabulary Band, and at almost 80 years of age is still marching with it on parades!

(Charles Troake)

116

Above. Constable 'Tiny' Turner operates a stirrup pump whilst Constable Hancox disinfects a motor car at a farm where an outbreak of 'Foot and Mouth' had occurred.

Below. Constables Stanley Pavey and Derek Harper, pictured at Lynton just after the disastrous floods of 15th August 1952. They were awarded the British Empire Medal and George Medal respectively for their heroic actions during that night when so many lives were lost, and the disaster itself remains one of the most significant peacetime events that the force had ever dealt with.

Above. The last helmet plate badge worn by officers of the Devon Constabulary up until its amalgamation into the Devon & Exeter Police. At that time the Devon Constabulary officers retained their old shoulder numbers for a few months and also kept the helmet plate badge of their old force until the new Devon & Cornwall Constabulary was created - although the Devon county helmet badge was still worn by some of the officers for several years after the amalgamation.

Above left. Pictured in the early 1960s, Constable Gary and Sergeant Joe Gater with their police dogs, Waldo and Feral, are seen here preparing to track an escaped convict from Dartmoor Prison. Sergeant Gater was one of the driving forces behind starting the police dog section (using loaned bloodhounds to track convicts) when he was a constable stationed at Bratton Clovelly, near Okehampton.

Left. Motor Patrol Constable 39 Fred Metters escorting an escaped convict called Bond into Okehampton Police Station in the December of 1957. Bond had been sentenced to death for murder, but was reprieved when hanging was abolished.

Constable Metters was stationed at Headquarters Traffic Department at Exeter, and was amongst other officers brought in when Bond escaped. These included Detective Sergeant Tom Pill, later a Chief Superintendent in the Devon & Cornwall force, who also appears in the photograph, standing at the rear.

(Retired Inspector Fred Metters)

EXETER CITY
Exeter City Police
(1836 - 1966)

The Exeter City Police was formed in 1836 as a result of the 'Municipal Corporation Act', but, initially, only as a 'day police'. Consequently an earlier system, whereby Exeter had been patrolled by three watchmen (unpaid) in each of the eight wards, had to remain in force during the night-time hours, a situation that continued for some years until the new city police became properly established. The first Headquarters was set up in the old guildhall; it was later moved to a new building in Waterbeer Street, and was to remain there until the opening of the present-day police station in the city.

As mentioned in the previous chapter, the Exeter City Police eventually amalgamated with the Devon Constabulary on 1st October 1966 to become the new Devon & Exeter Constabulary. At that time this was considered to be a 'trial run' for the more ambitious plan of joining the counties of Devon and Cornwall, along with the cities of Plymouth and Exeter, to form a new and considerably larger force in the Westcountry. This change also resulted in Mr Greenwood, the Chief Constable of the Devon Constabulary, taking charge of the new force and Mr Steer, the Exeter City Chief Constable, retiring soon afterwards. In addition, the area of the Exeter City Police became a division of the Devon & Exeter Constabulary.

Exeter City Police senior officers and sergeants, circa 1880. This photograph shows that the senior officers as well as the sergeants wore helmets at this time, although their frock coats were more ornate, and also that the sergeants (in common with many other forces of the day) wore chevrons only on the right sleeves of their tunics. Note also that beside each of their collar numbers is found the 'castle' emblem which was retained by the city police throughout its life.

Left. Chief Inspector Skinner of the city force, pictured in the late 1880s and, at that time, still wearing a helmet (see the next caption).

Chief Inspector Skinner's father had also been a police officer in Exeter some years earlier.

Below left. An inspector of the city force photographed in the 1890s, by which time the senior officers had adopted the pill box hat. This, in fact, was the usual head wear for senior officers in most police forces.

The city crest displayed on his hat was used in a variety of styles by the Exeter City Police. However, in a similar manner to the Devon Constabulary, the Exeter force did not adopt the use of the star style helmet plate badge.

Below right. A constable of the Exeter City Police with his wife, pictured in about 1890. On the left cuff of his tunic he is wearing a 'duty band' with horizontal stripes as opposed to the more common vertically striped one of the Metropolitan Police style.

Above. A traction engine accident in Fore Street, Exeter, on 25th April 1906. Luckily, despite the location, no injuries resulted from this incident.

Below. An unfortunate accident involving a tram on 7th March 1917 - regrettably two people were killed after apparently having been thrown from the vehicle's top deck. As can be seen, the incident attracted great crowds of spectators and, in fact, this particular photograph was on sale in the city within hours.

A modern-day police officer might do well to consider what effect the trauma of attending such an accident might have had without the availability of counselling services that are on hand for members of the emergency services nowadays.

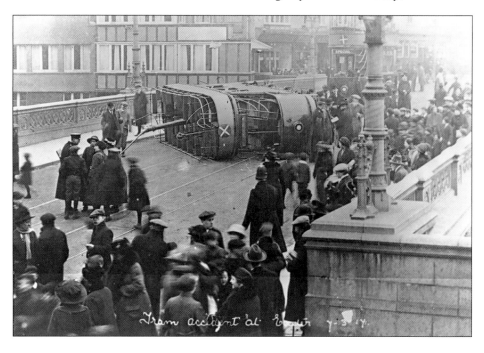

Left. Many city forces, nationally, adopted the use of a mounted section and Exeter was no exception, as can be seen from this photograph taken in the 1920s.

The photograph also shows that, by now, the style of the helmets had changed in a similar way to those of many other forces in the 1920s, the high ornate ball having been replaced by a low cloth dome. In addition, the 'castle crest' is now seen relocated to the epaulette and, instead, a crown is situated next to the collar number.

Below. Constable 25 Randle, pictured in about 1922 helping to start a 'mile of pennies' for a charitable event in the city. The 1920s style of helmet is shown well, although this was soon to be replaced in favour of the former, slightly more ornate, helmet with high ball top.

Exeter City Police, like the Devon Constabulary retained a crown on the collar for some years.

Below. A city sergeant pictured at around the time of the Great War, before the loss of the ornate high ball-topped helmet. The Exeter City crest on the helmet was a slightly different style, but, again, the crest was used as the helmet badge. Also, by this time the sergeants wore chevrons on both sleeves, in addition to the St. John's First Aid badge on the right.

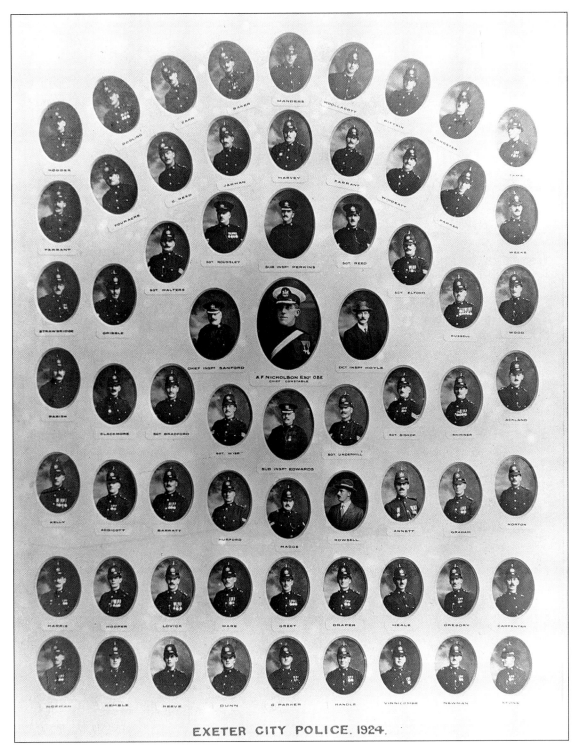

Exeter City Police 1924. This composition shows the whole of the Exeter City Police pictured in a huge frame. A rare example, as no other Westcountry force seems to have gone to such trouble, it is, perhaps, lasting proof of the pride and identity felt by the Exeter City officers.

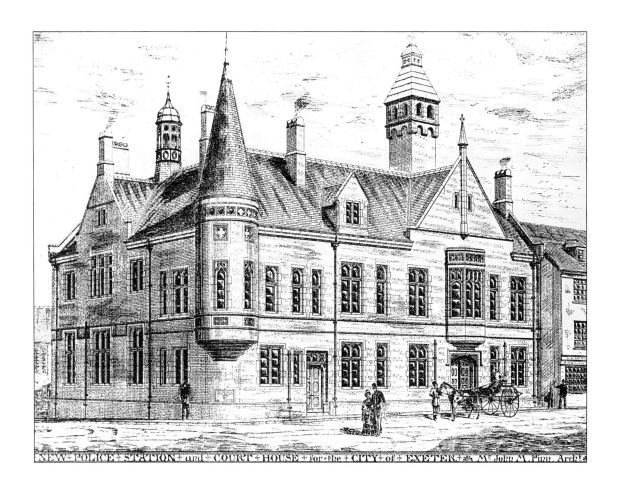

Above. An artist's impression of the new Exeter City Police Headquarters in Waterbeer Street, in the city centre. This fine building put to an end the rather cramped conditions under which the force had operated in the old guildhall, and remained its Headquarters until the late 1950s, when Heavitree Road Police Station was constructed.

Left. The first police vehicle in the Exeter force was this 'Utility Van', used for carrying emergency equipment, circa 1934. Clearly the contents show that the Exeter City Police was also a combined police and fire brigade like many other police forces at that time.

The officer with the vehicle is a constable of the newly-formed Traffic Division. His collar number has been relocated to the epaulette.

Above. Exeter City Police First Aid Team, photographed in the early 1930s with the regional trophy. First Aid played an important role in the police service, and involved officers sitting their St. John's First Aid exams and regularly taking part in competitions.

Below. Constable Arthur Dooling giving some timely road safety advice to a young cyclist. He is seen here at the Blackboy Road junction with Polsloe Road, in the Mount Pleasant district of the city.

(Richard Brooking-Smith)

Above. A rather extraordinary picture of some officers displaying their traffic directing abilities.

This scene may well draw a smile from a more modern-day officer, but directing traffic, as well as point duty, in the 1930s represented an important part of patrolling an officer's beat.

Left. Constable Fred Bennett, pictured in about 1932. Constable Bennett eventually achieved the rank of an inspector in the city force but, regrettably, some years after this photograph was taken, he was found collapsed in a street whilst on duty, and died on the spot.

On hearing of his death, a tramp in Bristol walked to Exeter to attend his funeral only to be told at the local police station that he was a day too late. He was, however, taken by a constable to Inspector Bennett's grave, where he laid some flowers. When asked why a tramp should want to do this, he replied that the inspector had never walked past him without giving him money for a meal - a fitting tribute to a popular and kind man from perhaps someone in a better position than many to see the full extent of this officer's compassion.

(Harold Bennett)

126

Above left. A Constable of the wartime city force, pictured in the early 1940s, with steel helmet and respirator. The routine duties of the police during the war years were increased tremendously, as they had to co-ordinate much of the rescue work undertaken by the civilian and military emergency services. In fact, police officers often went for days on duty with little or no sleep in conditions which their modern-day colleagues would find intolerable.

Above right. War Reserve Constable 192 Henry Lyle, who served in the Exeter City War Reserve Police from 1943 to 1948. Although the war ended in 1945 many of these officers remained in the police service to assist in the post-war years, some serving up until the 1950s. The war reserve officers had "WR" on their collars and, despite not wearing helmets, had the same powers as a regular constable.

(Mrs Sylvia Payne)

Right. A belt buckle, helmet plate and 'collar dogs' of the Exeter City Police.

(Dave Wilkinson)

Exeter in the Blitz, 1943. A constable and inspector visit the scene of what used to be the top end of Paris Street. In many respects the blitz on Exeter was just as terrible as that on Plymouth, but fortunately many of the old buildings survived thereby enabling the city to retain much of its unique character.

Above. Pictured in the early 1940s, this young man is pushing an 'Easter Egg' advertising a local egg producer.

Below. Sergeant Sangster and Constable Ware of the Exeter City Police mounted section, photographed in 1946.

Left. The use of 'Police Boxes', mainly in city force areas, was quite common. This one was situated on the main road to Taunton and is typical of the 1940s style.

Police boxes provided the public with a telephone in a small cupboard for emergency use, as well as a degree of 'sanctuary' for the patrolling beat officer. A small table and chair usually comprised the only furniture, which the officer used whilst on his beat for report writing and also for refreshment breaks.

Below. The Traffic Division, seen in the late 1940s in the rear yard of the Waterbeer Street Headquarters of the Exeter City Police. The van seen here is the general purpose utility vehicle, and the officer standing second from right is the sergeant in charge of the department. Also to be seen, in the background, is the distinctive turret at the front of the station building.

An inspection by His Majesty's Inspector of Constabulary, Mr Johnston, in 1952. Pictured in the Civic Hall, Exeter, he is accompanied by the Chief Constable, Mr A. E. Rowsell, and Chairman of the Watch Committee, Mr P. Slader. In the foreground are Women Police Constables Glanville and Woolridge.

(The Western Morning News Co. Ltd.)

Above. Sergeants Frank Ware and Nick Carter (nearest the camera), pictured in the 1960s in the Traffic Department office at Exeter. A photograph of Sergeant Ware also appears on page 129, showing him several years earlier as a constable in the mounted section.

Left. Constable Peter Nordqvist, seen at the Paris Street police pillar (at the junction with Heavitree Road) shortly before the 1966 amalgamation of the Exeter City Police with the Devon Constabulary to form the Devon & Exeter Police. These police pillars gradually superseded the former police boxes and were used on city beats before the days of the personal radio. They provided a telephone connection to the police station, for the public as well as for police officers, and were also used as a fixed point for the sergeant to meet the patrolling constable on the beat.

On the top of the pillar was a light which was automatically illuminated when the telephone rang. This drew the attention of the patrolling constable to the fact that a colleague at the police station was trying to contact him.

132

Devon & Exeter Police
(1966 - 1967)

The shortest lived police force in the Westcountry survived from 1st October 1966 until 1st June 1967, a matter of just eight months. Nevertheless, the amalgamation of the Devon Constabulary and the Exeter City Police, from which it was created, resulted in some important lessons being learned prior to the amalgamation with the Cornwall Constabulary and Plymouth City Police that followed in the June of 1967. Without this 'trial run' the formation of the Devon & Cornwall Constabulary would, indeed, have been far less smooth than proved to be the case.

During this 'interim' period uniforms remained essentially unchanged, for there was no point in incurring such expense for the sake of a few months; but a new force crest was adopted and used on police vehicles and badges. The officer-in-charge, throughout, was Mr Greenwood, the Chief Constable of the former Devon Constabulary, and it was he who steered the force through these significant changes.

The cap badge of the Devon & Exeter Police. It was only the officers of the Special Constabulary who actually wore the crest as a cap badge as the regular officers (who used them as 'collar dogs') tended to retain either the Devon Constabulary or Exeter City Police badge, depending on which force they had joined, while new recruits were usually issued with a Devon Constabulary cap badge.

The Hatherleigh Section Special Constabulary. This photograph, taken in the mid-1960s prior to the section's disbandment, clearly shows that the 'regular' section sergeant (seated and wearing the broad chevrons) has a Devon Constabulary cap badge whereas all the other officers, being 'specials', have the new 'Devon & Exeter' one.

Right. Police cadets of the Devon & Exeter Police, pictured at the Dartmoor Training Centre. The cadet in the foreground has the Exeter City Police 'collar dog' badges on both his epaulettes, but his colleague does not. This would suggest that he was from Heavitree Road Police Station in the city of Exeter, and his companion was a cadet posted elsewhere in the county.

Below. An inspection taking place in the quadrangle of the Headquarters building at Exeter. Inspector 'Tony' Southern is pictured with the Cornwall Constabulary crest 'collar dogs' as he had originally joined that force.

Left. Inspector Ken Reid, pictured when he was stationed at Tavistock in 1966. He is seen here wearing the 'collar dogs' of the Devon & Exeter Police, although he is wearing Devon Constabulary buttons.

(Jim Thorrington)

Below. Motor Patrol Constable 377 Roger Jones, seen standing beside his Mark III Ford Zephyr at Yelverton, in 1966. He was based at Plymstock in the Plympton Traffic Section area, and at this time the motor patrol officers would wear the initials 'MP' on their epaulette, above their 'collar number'.

Constable Jones recalls that due to the light weight of the rear of these patrol cars (which carried the crest of the Devon & Exeter Police on their doors) they would easily swerve when on a pursuit, so it was decided that a 'technical' modification was needed to improve their stability. The upshot was that after he'd 'found' a concrete kerbstone from 'somewhere', and placed it in the boot, the car's roadholding was transformed to such an extent that, by all accounts, the idea was adopted by many other motor patrol officers at the time!

(Roger Jones)

The Devon & Cornwall Constabulary
(1967 - 2000)

The final amalgamation in the Westcountry took place on 1st June 1967, when, at last, the plans for one single police force came to fruition. No longer would there be an Exeter or Plymouth City Police, nor would the two counties of Devon and Cornwall be separate constabularies.

Such a significant change obviously took some months to come into full effect, and even longer for the more "parochially minded" officer to accept. Indeed, many years would pass before the uniform of the Devon & Cornwall Constabulary would be the sole uniform worn in the Westcountry: like the alteration from blue shirts to white for constables and sergeants that was to follow in 1979, there was a degree of reluctance to change. Many hurdles were overcome, however, and the current force has adapted and evolved to meet the demands of an ever-changing society.

The Armorial Bearings of The Devon & Cornwall Police Authority.

The Shield: This combines the elements from the Arms of Devon and Cornwall County Councils with a reference to police work. The waves are common to both arms in reference to the peninsular position. The red lion from the Devon arms is that of Richard Plantagenet, Earl of Cornwall, who bore it within a black border charged with 15 bazants or gold roundels. The black area and the bazants appear in the Cornwall arms. Richard's lion wore a gold crown; this is replaced by a crown 'Vallary' i.e. with points resembling the pales of a stockade which, coloured blue, suggests the security afforded by the police authority.

The Crest: The 'crown vallary' contains a half length figure of one of the gold lions which support the Plymouth arms, furnished with the white and blue barred wings of Exeter's pegasi, and wearing, at the neck, its blue naval crown, recalling the long connections of the area with the Royal Navy.

Motto. 'For the Assistance of All'. This expresses the role of the police in the community, and is a combination of the Devon motto - 'Auxilio Divino' (Sir Francis Drake's motto - 'With Divine Help') and that of Cornwall - 'One and All'.

Above. One of the first 'Unit Beat' policing vehicles used by the force was the Morris Minor, in its distinctive white and blue 'panda' colours. The officer here is wearing the first issue of Devon & Cornwall Constabulary helmets, which was the old Devon county helmet with the new star badge helmet plate.

Left. Constable Dennis Smith. Any story of the Devon & Cornwall Constabulary would be incomplete without the account of the courage and devotion to duty displayed by Constable Smith, which were in the highest tradition of the police service. The only officer of the force to be shot and killed in the execution of his duty, he was posthumously awarded the Queen's Police Medal for gallantry.

He was shot at Torquay a few days before Christmas 1973 by one Martin Fenton, whose vehicle he had stopped whilst on routine patrol. Fenton then stole Constable Smith's police vehicle to make his get-away before going into an Exeter casino, where he shot and killed three more men. Later, Fenton was convicted of four murders and sentenced to life imprisonment; he subsequently died behind bars.

Right. One of the most baffling of disappearances that has occurred in the Westcountry - the case of Genette Tate. Genette was a 13 year-old schoolgirl who was delivering newspapers in her village of Aylesbeare, not far from Exeter, on Saturday, 19th August 1978 when she went missing. Her bicycle was found lying in the road by two girls who had been walking down the lane with her just minutes earlier.

Genette's disappearance sparked one of the largest and prolonged enquiries undertaken by the Devon & Cornwall Constabulary, and was one which attracted massive national interest. Hundreds of posters, such as the one shown on the right, were distributed and displayed all over the South West, but over 20 years later little is known about what happened to her.

(Express and Echo Publications Ltd.)

Below. Hundreds of members of the public came forward as a result of an appeal for support to assist the police in searching the nearby Woodbury Common. In this photograph Inspector Mike Hooper, in uniform, is joined, on his left, by Mr John Alderson, the Chief Constable. Mr Alderson was most insistent that he did not wish to take command of that search team, but wanted to do all that he could, like many hundreds of other concerned individuals, to help in the search.

(Express and Echo Publications Ltd.)

DEVON AND CORNWALL CONSTABULARY

MISSING GIRL

HAVE YOU SEEN GENETTE

SHORTLY after 3.30 p.m. on Saturday, August 19th, Genette Tate, aged 13, vanished from a country lane in the East Devon village of Aylesbeare. Minutes earlier she had been cycling along Within Road on her evening newspaper round. She stopped to talk with two friends, then rode off out of sight . . .

THAT WAS THE LAST ANYONE SAW OF GENETTE

THREE hundred yards further on, her friends found her abandoned bike, lying on its side with newspapers scattered about the lane. There was no sign of a struggle. The rider had simply disappeared. Within the space of ten minutes Genette had vanished without trace.

- Massive searches involving police, tracker dogs, Royal Marines, helicopters and thousands of volunteers have failed to unearth a single clue as to Genette's whereabouts.
- Extensive press and T.V. coverage throughout this country and overseas has proved fruitless.
- The offer of large rewards produce no positive information.

Genette is 5ft. tall, with short brown wavy hair and brown eyes. She was wearing a white cotton top with her name embroidered in red on the left shoulder, light brown trousers and white plimsolls.

RECONSTRUCTION

IF YOU HAVE SEEN GENETTE OR CAN THROW ANY LIGHT ON THIS MYSTERY PLEASE TELEPHONE THE POLICE AT EXETER (0392) 33399 OR CONTACT ANY POLICE STATION IMMEDIATELY

Above. During the mid-1970s the whole style and ethos of policing the Westcountry went over to the principals of 'community policing', with the Chief Constable, John Alderson, being in the forefront of this idea nationally. A 'community friendship week' was organised each year in May and involved various events to bring the public and police closer together.

In this photograph, taken in about 1977 at Falmouth, the Chief Constable (on the left) is joined by the singer, Joe Brown, at such an event. On the right is pictured the rather formidable Chief Inspector 'Gerry' Tremelling, whilst Woman Constable Janet Dolling looks on.

Left. Members of the underwater search unit seen on their launch providing security for the Royal Yacht at Dartmouth. Sergeant Dave Ellis on the right is at the helm.

(Supt. Dave Ellis)

Right. The 1978 'Barbarian' Rugby match at Camborne met a great deal of opposition because of the apartheid problems in South Africa. Demonstrations took place and the rugby match needed a large police presence to keep order.

Owing to a lack of available official transport, the police officers were paraded in the road outside the police station and marched, in a large contingent, to the rugby ground. As it happened, the 'heavens opened': this great downpour lasted for most of the match, and seemed to reduce the risk of any potential aggression.

After the match ended, the rather wet police officers were marched back to Camborne Police Station, where they were issued with dry trousers from Divisional Stores!

Left. Police Support Unit training in 1978. Following instances of civil unrest and rioting, particularly in the inner cities, training for such disorder took on a more formal nature. This early photograph of training indicates how primitive the equipment was in the initial years. Football shin pads and cricket boxes were the order of the day, as opposed to the high-tech equipment available now.

Above. The Devon & Cornwall Constabulary, always keen to enhance community relations, was supported by the sponsorship of Barclays Bank, who originally funded 'PC Padlock'. He is still a frequent visitor to charitable events and fetes throughout the force area, spreading the community policing word.

Below. The miners' dispute of 1983/84 saw the relationship between the public and the police stretched to the limit. This picture, taken at a Derbyshire colliery, shows clearly the officers of the Devon & Cornwall Constabulary in their distinctive yellow reflective coats - which earned them the nickname of 'Daffodils'. Forces from all over the country provided support to the Derbyshire police, in a similar manner to the assistance given to the Cornwall Constabulary during the clay workers' strikes at St. Austell in 1913, and the officers of the Devon & Cornwall Constabulary acquitted themselves in an exemplary manner throughout this challenging time.

Above. The Band of the Devon & Cornwall Constabulary, pictured in 1998 at Porthleven. This band, formed in the mid-1970s, has raised thousands of pounds for various charities and consists of retired as well as serving members of the force. The 78 year-old retired Constable Charles Troake (see page 116) can be seen playing the cymbals behind the 'Corps of Drums'.

Below. This is the third helicopter which the force has used since the early 1980s. With a force area larger than most, and a huge coastline and moorland area to police, the helicopter has become an essential tool in the fight against crime, as well as saving countless lives when called to support the other emergency services in the force area.

Above. Forging closer links with other agencies has proved beyond doubt that the problems of crime can be tackled with greater effectiveness. One example is that of working together with the Dartmoor National Park Ranger Service, as pictured here, for this has led to the problem of theft from vehicles on Dartmoor being greatly reduced.

The Devon & Cornwall Constabulary move into a new millennium committed to the principal that by working in partnership with the local community we can all take responsibility for tackling the problems of crime and disorder.

Thank you for your support in purchasing this book. The profits from its sales are being donated to the Widows and Orphans Compassionate Fund charity which does so much good to help those bereaved families of colleagues, both past and present.

Through the photographic story told in these pictures it is hoped that the reader will go away enlightened as to how we, in the Devon & Cornwall Constabulary, have developed our style of policing; a style which, as already mentioned, is not only the envy of many British police forces, but also others worldwide.

Throughout our existence (since the final amalgamations in 1967, which created the Devon & Cornwall Constabulary), we have gone through many changes to meet the demands of the community we serve. We have often had to look at the examples of the past to see the best way forward in an ever-changing society; and, hopefully, these photographs will leave you with a greater understanding of how we have evolved since the dawn of the British policing system. Perhaps, too, the reader will now understand why so many young men and women wish to wear the uniform of a British police officer with a sense of pride. We are, however, as often said throughout this book, citizens, policing with the public's consent and with their support. As we approach a new millennium it is to the public that we now turn, with closer multi-agency approaches to tackling the problems of crime and disorder. What that new millennium has in store for the police service in the Westcountry is anybody's guess, but one thing will be for sure:-

' Tempora mutantur, et nos mutamur in illis'
(Times change, and we change with them)